Imagician

Carl Lyle Jenkins

Imagician

Visionary Paintings
and
Photography

By

Carl Lyle Jenkins

Santa Fe, NM

2016

Also by Carl Lyle Jenkins

Question Reality!

The Legend of Baldohr--A Forest Dream

Battlelines

Ratlantis--The Rise and Fall of the Rat Race Part 1

Secrets of the Laughing Wave

Why?

"Well, Art is Art, isn't it?

Still, on the other hand, water is water.

And east is east and west is west
and if you take cranberries and stew them like applesauce
they taste much more like prunes than rhubarb does.

Now tell me what you know."

~~Groucho Marx~~

Artist's Statement

The images herein are a partial portfolio of my oil and acrylic paintings, photographs, and digitally created artworks mostly produced over the last fifteen to 20 years.

Most people have at least some understanding concerning painting and photography. While more familiar to most than when I first started using it nearly 20 years ago, some folks may still consider the digital imaging/photo collage process a bit mysterious. For the uninitiated, a little explanation concerning how the process works may help.

 When using a computer, the artist is literally painting with light, using programming tools that enable the creation of images visualized on a digital monitor. I find that working in this medium stretches my imagination and creativity to their outermost limits. All tools used with more conventional mediums—and many that are unique to computers—are available to the digital artist. Using a mouse or a graphics tablet and stylus, I select from a wide variety of types, shapes and sizes of brushes, airbrushes, palette knives, pencils, pens, and erasers. The colours with which I paint are selected from an infinite palette and mixed within the computer.

Some of my digital paintings are created entirely within virtual reality. Other images incorporate paintings and drawings I create outside the computer—as well as my original photographs--which are imported into the computer from the camera or by using a scanner. The imported art and photography are then incorporated into the digital painting using a layering process. Layers are stacked one on top of another like sheets of glass. They are then digitally manipulated. Opacity, contrast, color, hue, and saturation may be altered in the individual layers. Various filters may be used to create special effects. The layers are then blended with one another using a variety of digital techniques. The final digital image is then typically rendered using a Giclee (inkjet) Printmaking process.

I truly hope you enjoy the selections from my work found herein.

Carl Lyle Jenkins

Santa Fe, New Mexico   January 2016

Catalogue of Images

1. Blue Buddha (Digital Image, 2005)

2. Mt. Clements, Glacier National Park, USA, (Photo, 2009)

3. Haleakala Dreaming--Birth of the Moon (Digital Image, 2002)

4. Falls From Heaven (Digital Image, 2000)

5. Rainforest Reflections (Digital Image, 2006)

6. Apache Mountain Spirit Dancer Returns (Digital Image, 2008)

7. Charley Young Beach (Digital Image, 2001)

8. Two Medicine Lake, Glacier National Park, USA (Photo, 2009)

9. Pecos River Rapids (Oil on Canvas, 24" x 30, 2008)

10. Flow (Oil on Canvas, triptych, 24" x 72", 2008)

11. Cloud Hidden (Oil on Canvas, 24" x 30", 2009)

12. Crossroads (Digital Image, 2010)

13. Magic Mirror (Digital Image, 2005)

14. Canyons (Oil on Canvas, 30" x 40", 2012)

15. Oomphala (Oil on Canvas, 18" x 24", 2007)

16. Blue Eyed Dream (Digital Image, 2012)

17. Lola Mae Bychu (Digital Image, 2000)

18. Higher Ground (Acrylic/Mixed Media on Canvas, 24" x 30", 2015)

19. Lanai (Oil on Canvas, 18" x 24", 1998)

20. Feathered Fantasy (Digital Image, 2000)

21. Fluertex (Digital Image, 2005)

22. Spring, Two Medicine Lake, Glacier National Park, USA (Photo, 2007)

23. Oahu Huhu (Digital Image, 2002)

24. Firedance (Acrylic Painting on Canvas, 36″ x 48″, 2012)

25. The River (Oil on Canvas, 24″ x 30″, 2012)

26. Janus (Digital Image, 2012)

27. Out of the Blue (Acrylic Painting on Masonite, 48″ x 48″, 2015)

28. Vista (Oil on Canvas, 24″ x 36″, 2012)

29. Threes (Digital Image, 2004)

30. Convergence (Acrylic Painting on Canvas, 5 panels, 40″ x 150″, 2015)

31. Paradise Point (Digital Image, 2001

32. The Visitation (Digital Image, 1999)

33. Dancing with Destiny (Digital Image, 2002)

34. Flamenco (Digital Image, 2002)

35. Secret Beach (Digital Image, 2001)

36. Pecos Ruins (Oil on Canvas, 18″ x 24″, 2008)

37. Nirvana (Digital Image, 2004)

38. Cloudy with a Chance of Sharks (Digital Image, 2014)

39. Thermal Pond, Yellowstone National Park (Photo, 2010)

40. Nightfire (Digital Image, 2000)

41. Los Luceros (Oil on Canvas, 30″ x 40″, 2008)

42. Kiss (Digital Image, 2007)

43. Funny Money (Digital Image, 1999)

44. Lost in the Crowd (Digital Image, 2002)

45. New Wave (Digital Image, 2006)

46. Near Ghost Ranch, Northern New Mexico (Photo, 2010)

47. Haleakala Dreaming—Snake of Self (Digital Image, 1998)

48. Near Jasper, Canada (Photo, 1989)

49. New Dimensions (Digital Image, 2005)

50. Mosquito Island, Lake St. Mary, Glacier National Park, USA (Photo, 2007)

51. Cascade (Digital Image, 2005)

52. Nightmare on the Plaza   (Digital Image, 2008)

53. Lahaina Luna (Digital Image, 2002)

54. Planet Dance (Digital Image, 2004)

55. Seven (Acrylic/Mixed Media on Masonite, 24" x 24", 2015)

56. Flowers From Pele (Oil on Canvas, 24" x 30", 1998)

57. I Shadow (Oil on Canvas, 18" x 24", 2008)

58. Pecos Wilderness (Oil on Canvas, 18" x 24", 2008)

59. Shiva (Digital Image, 2010)

60. Gallery (Acrylic/Mixed Media on Canvas, 30" x 40", 2014)

61. Summer, Two Medicine Lake, Glacier National Park, USA (Photo, 2010)

62. Corridor (Digital Image 2014)

63. Square Dancer (Digital Image, 2014)

64. Spooky Night (Digital Image, 2014)

65. Dragonfly's Dream (Digital Image, 2006)

66. Fabled and Forbidden Lands (Digital Image, 2015)

67. Desert Sands (Oil on Canvas, 30" x 40", 2010)

68. Santa Cruz (Oil on Canvas, 24" x 36", 1977)

69. Pecos River (Oil on Canvas, 24" x 30", 2008)

70. Fall (Oil on Canvas, 30" x 30", 2007)

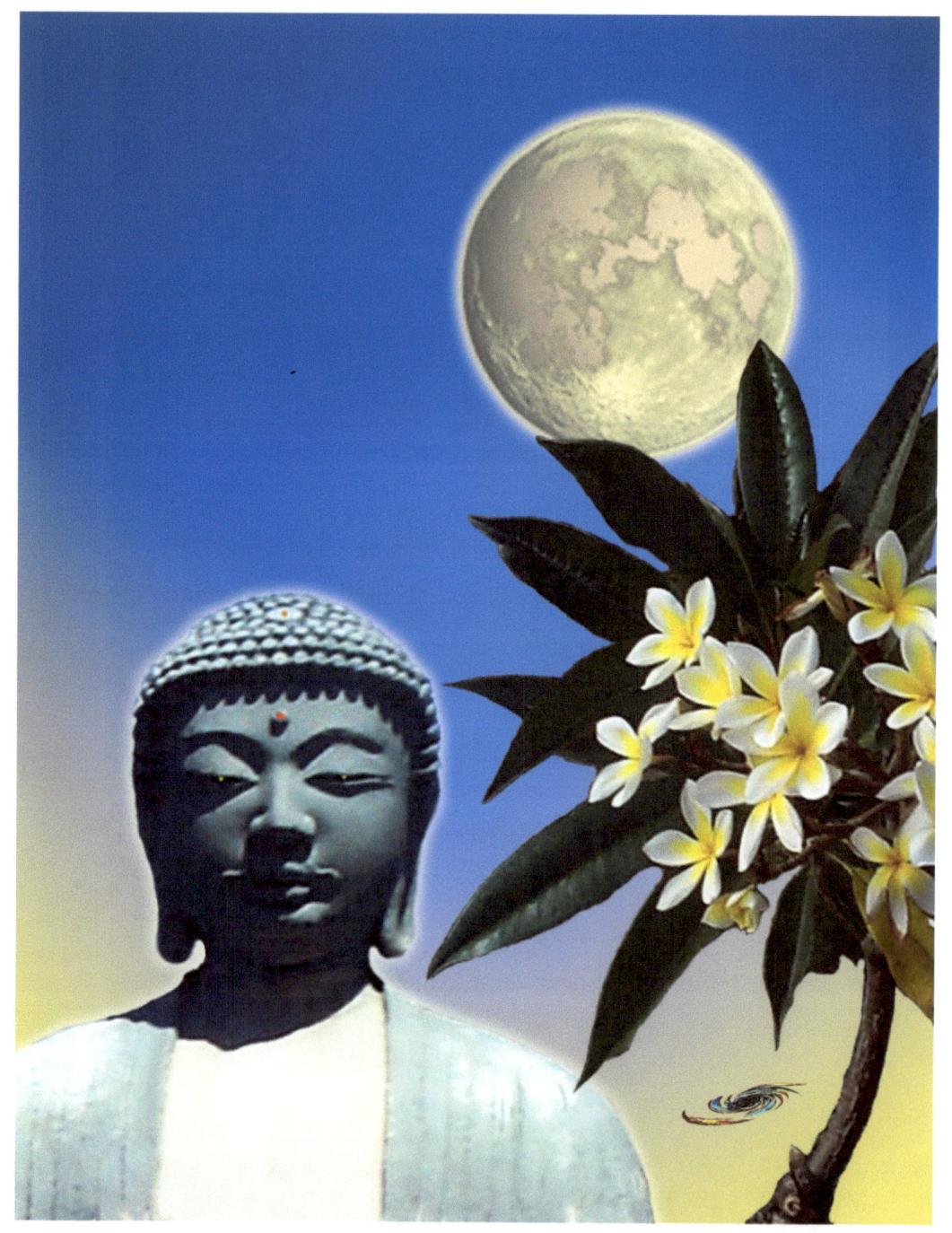

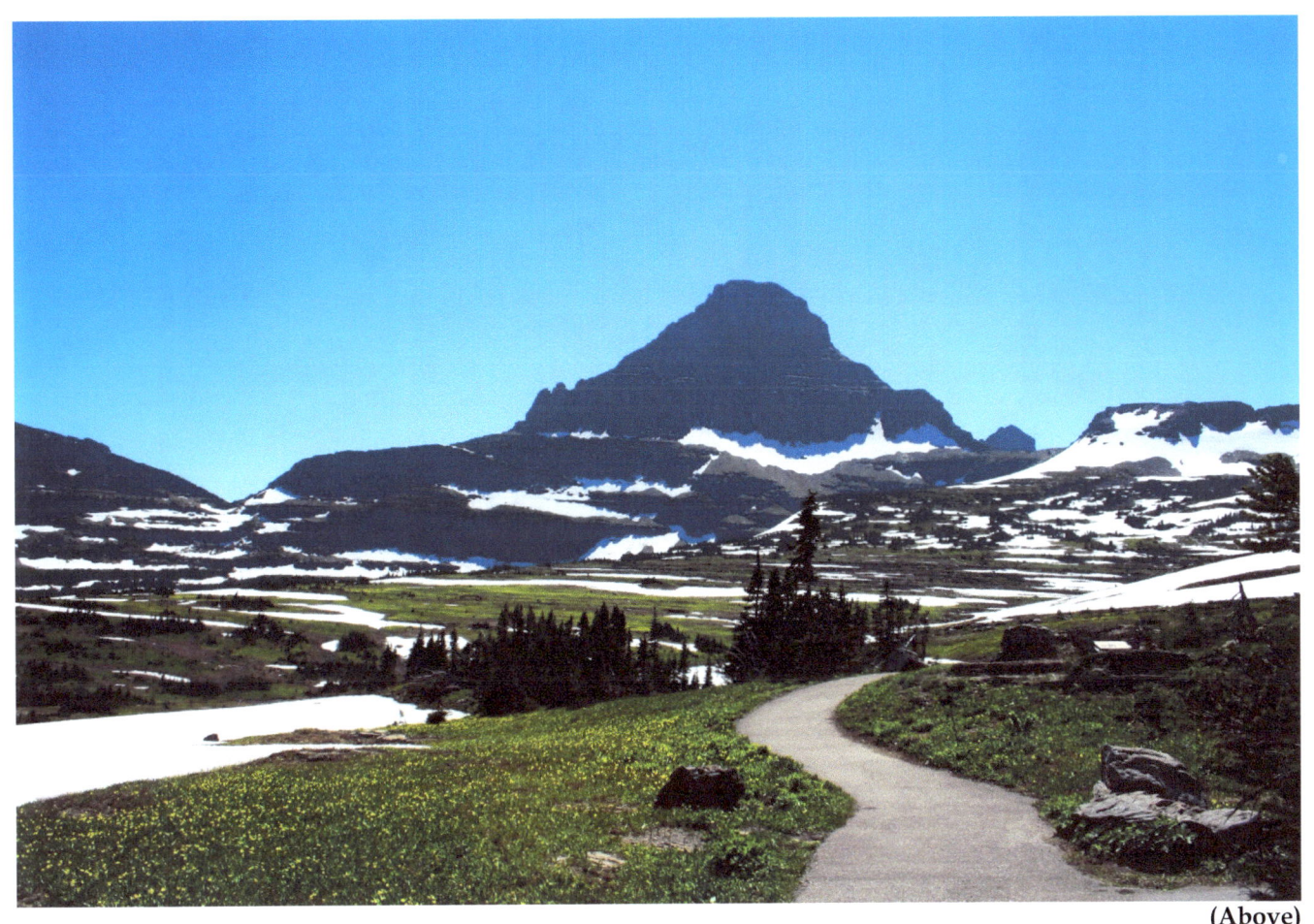

(Above)

2. Mt. Clements, Glacier National Park, USA (Photo, 2009)

(Left)

1. Blue Buddha (Digital Image, 2005)

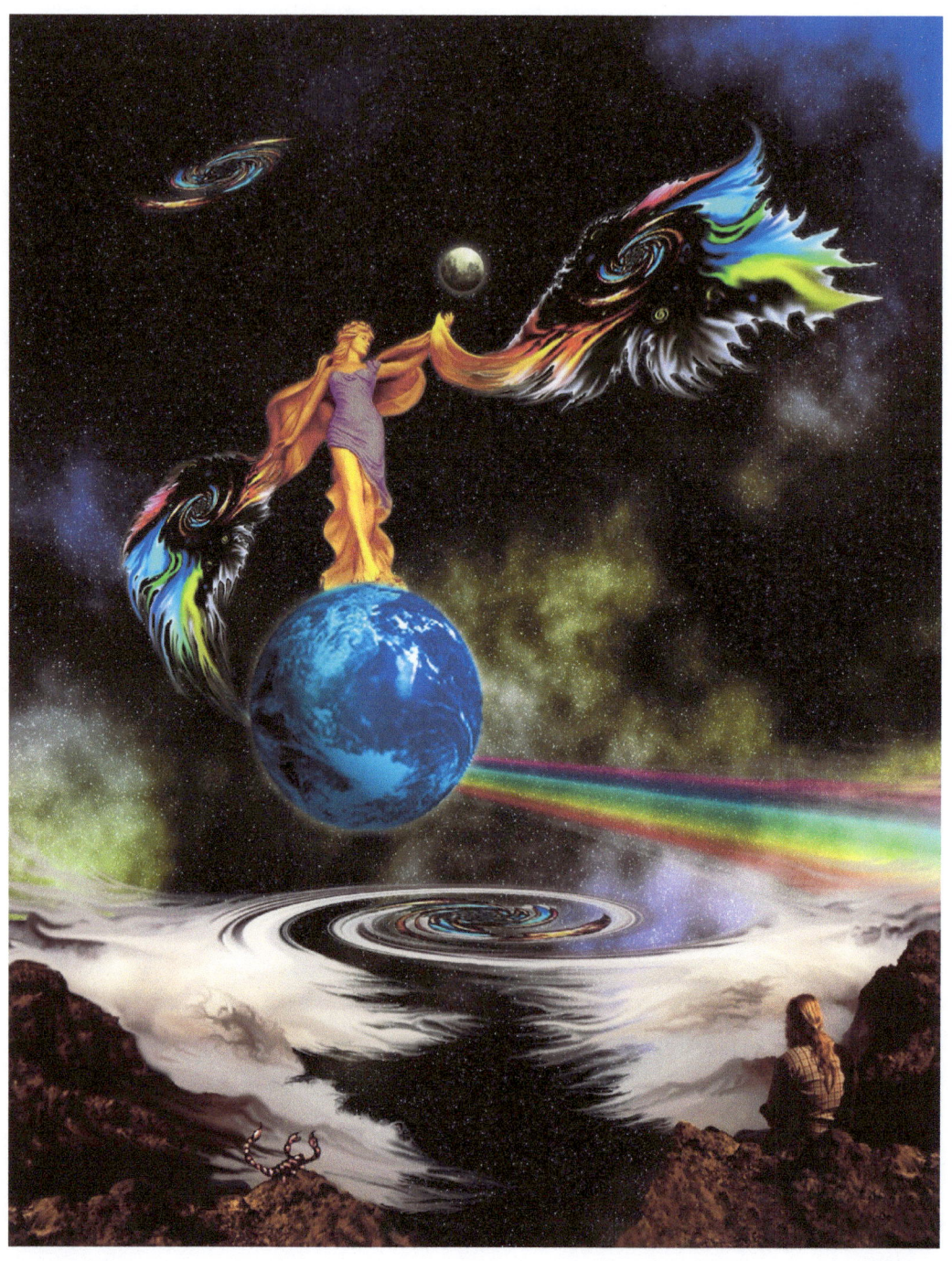

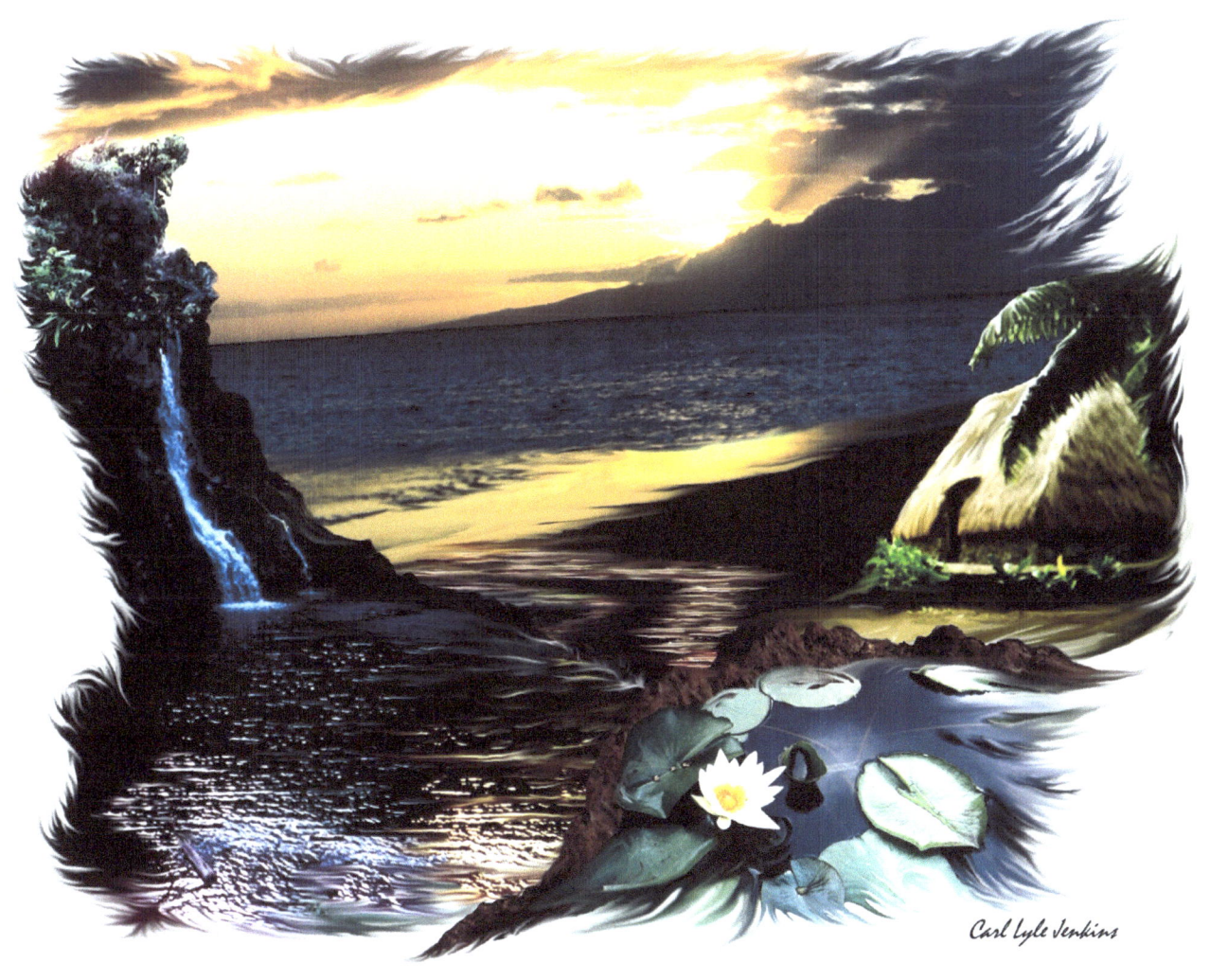

Carl Lyle Jenkins

4. *Falls From Heaven* (Digital Image, 2000)

3. *Haleakala Dreaming--Birth of the Moon* (Digital Image, 2002)

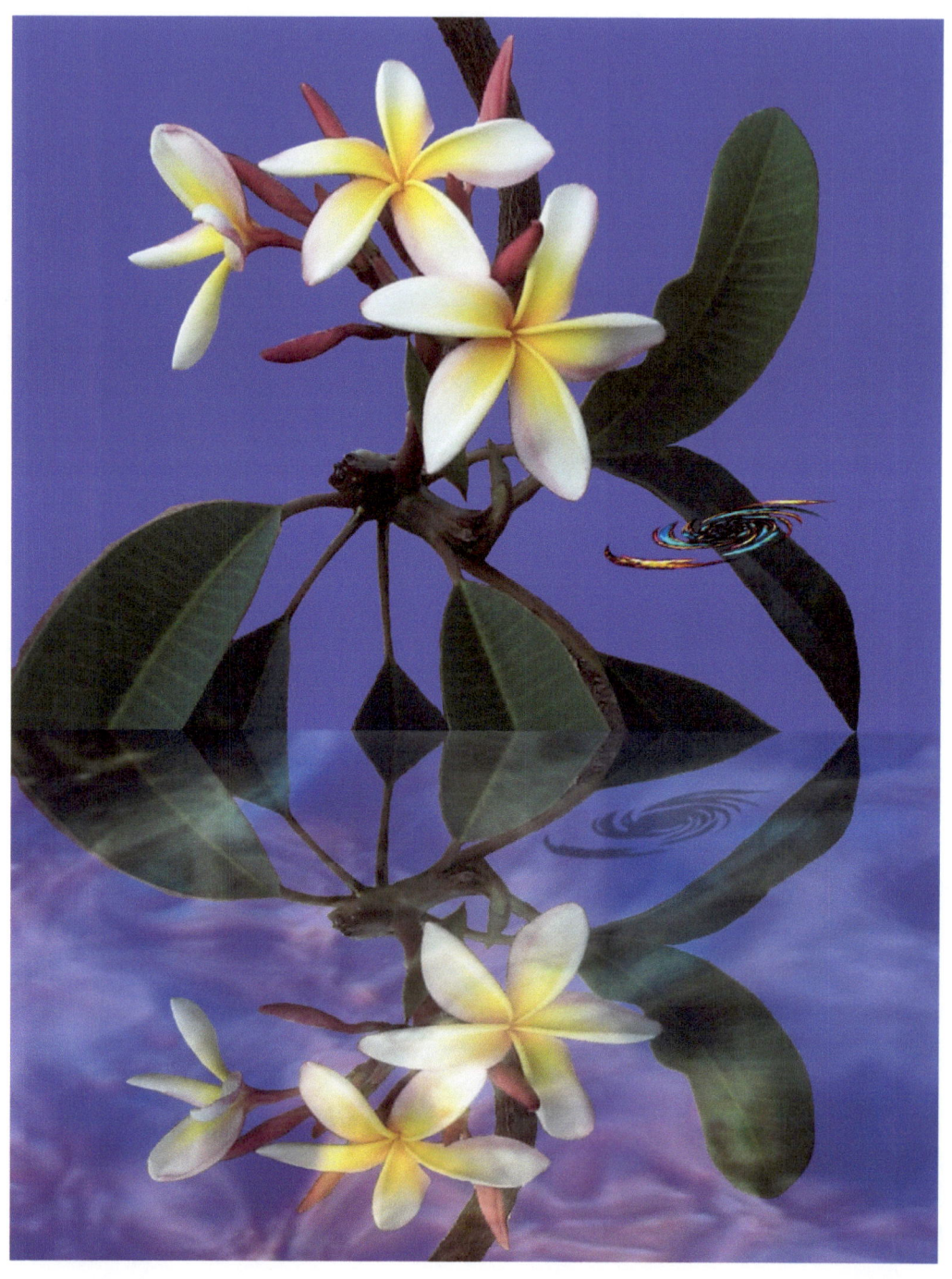

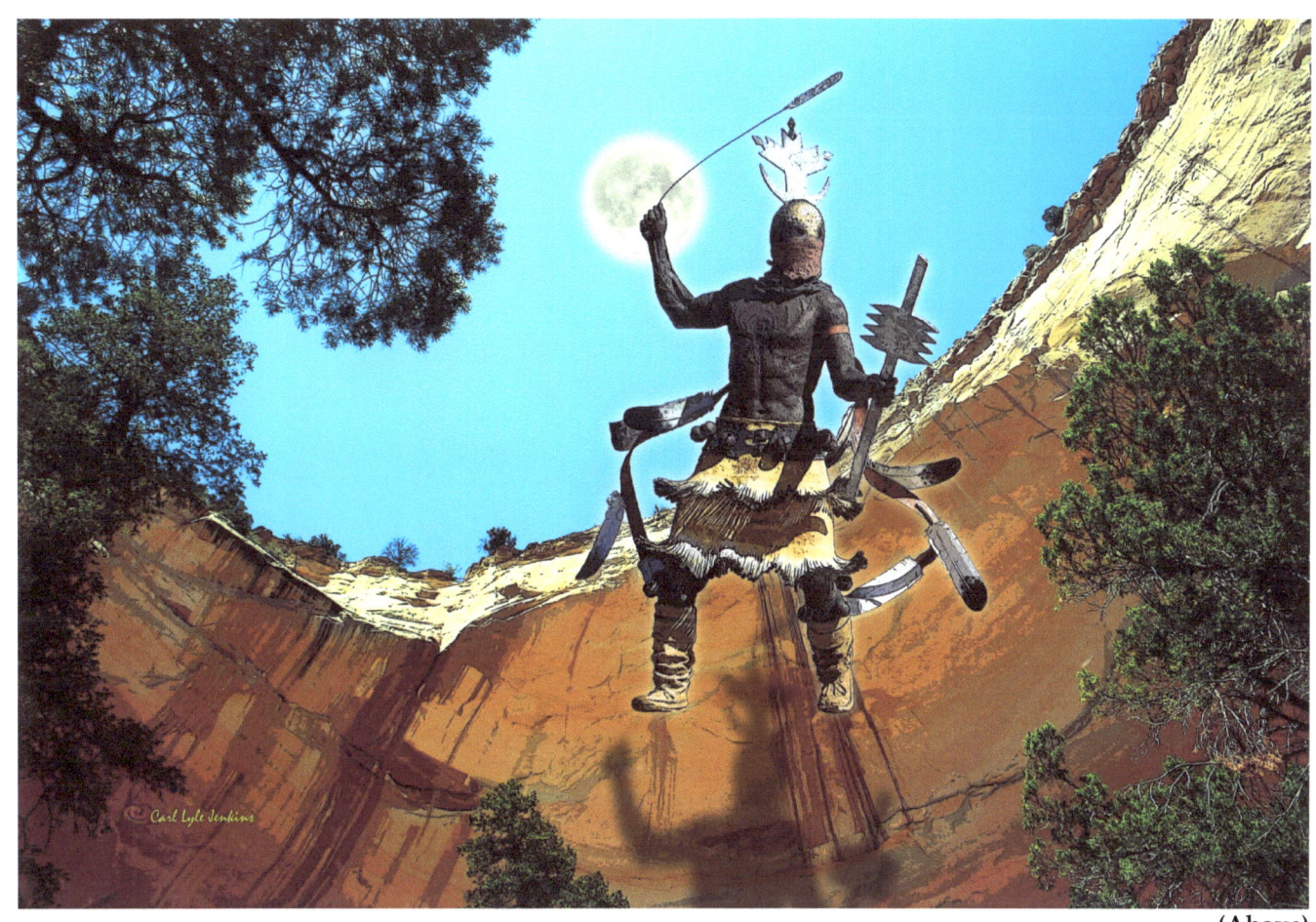

6. *Apache Mountain Spirit Dancer Returns* (Digital Image, 2008)

5. *Rainforest Reflections* (Digital Image, 2006)

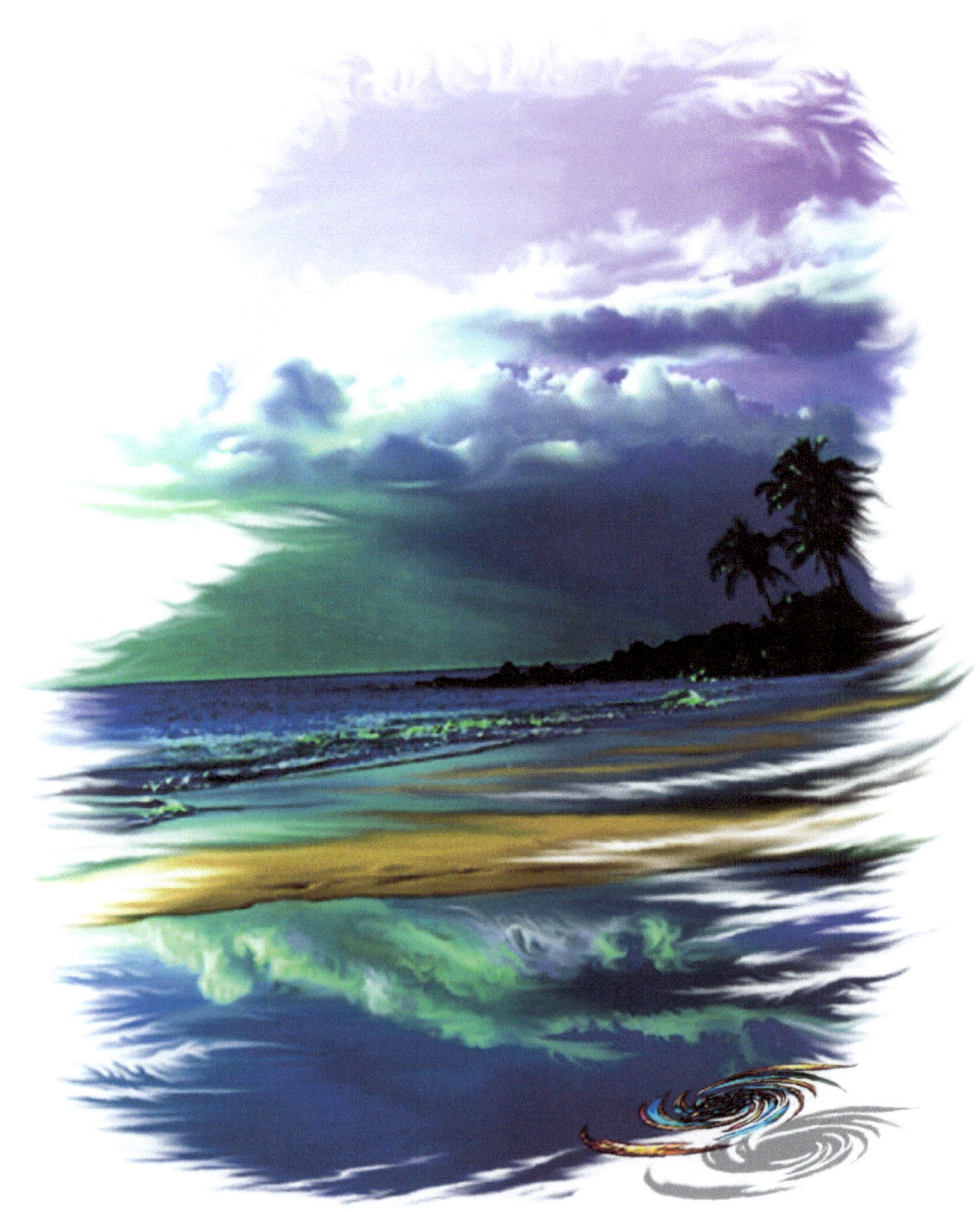

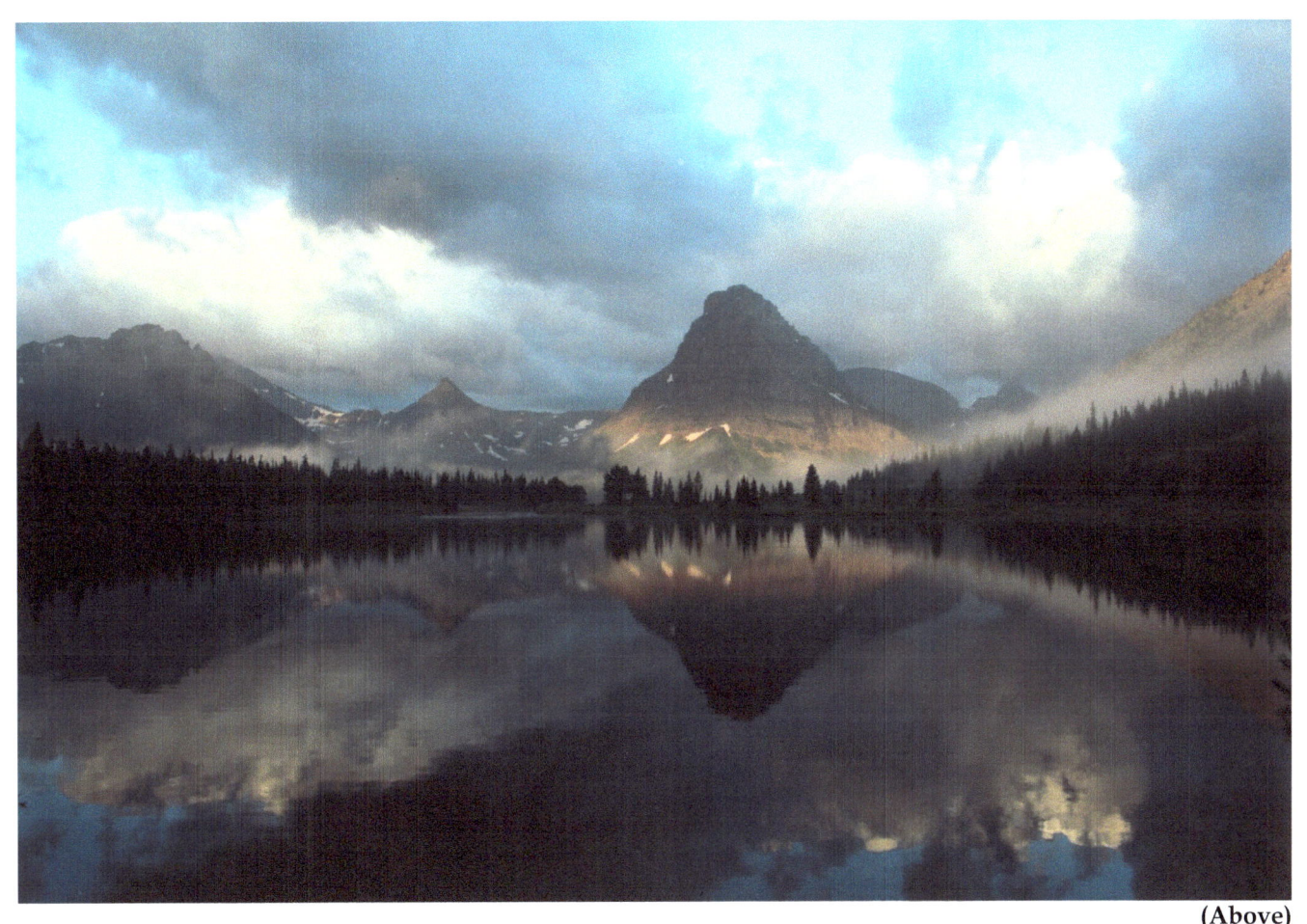

(Above)

8. Two Medicine Lake, Glacier National Park, USA (Photo, 2009)

(Left)

7. Charley Young Beach (Digital Image, 2001)

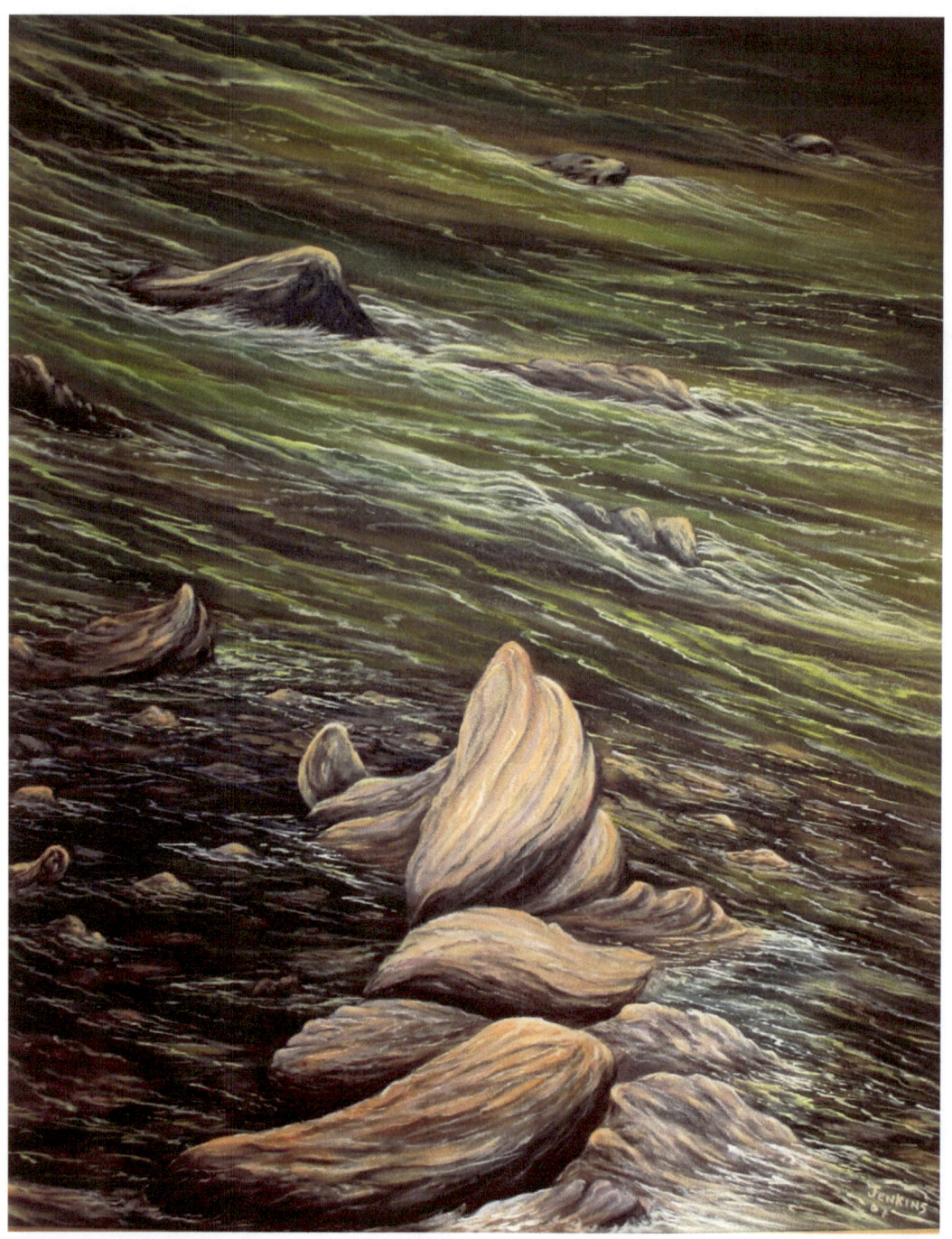

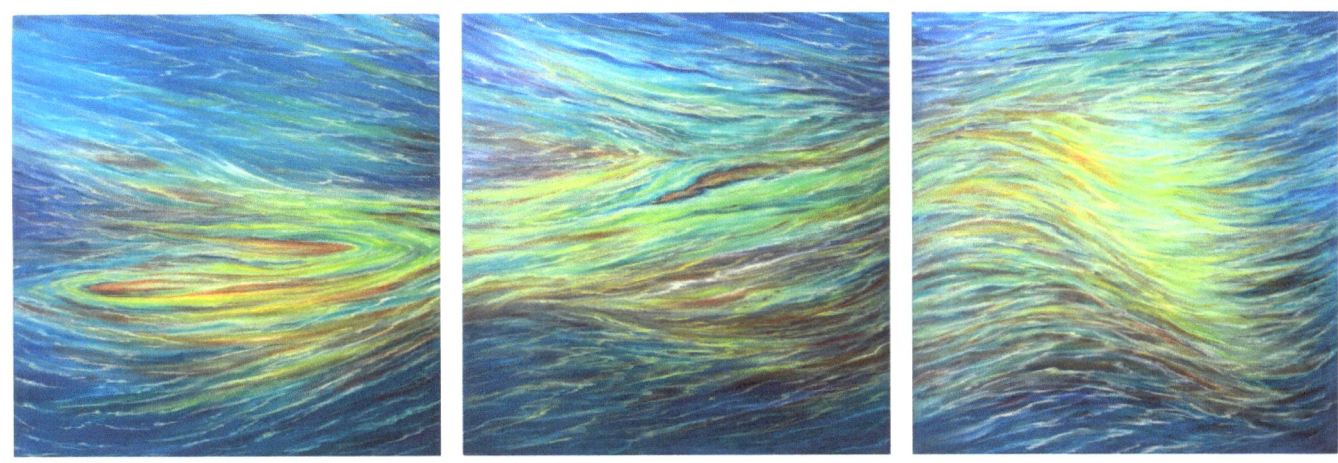

(Above)

10. Flow (Oil on Canvas, triptych, 24″ x 72″, 2008)

(Left)

9. Pecos River Rapids (Oil on Canvas, 24″ x 30″, 2008)

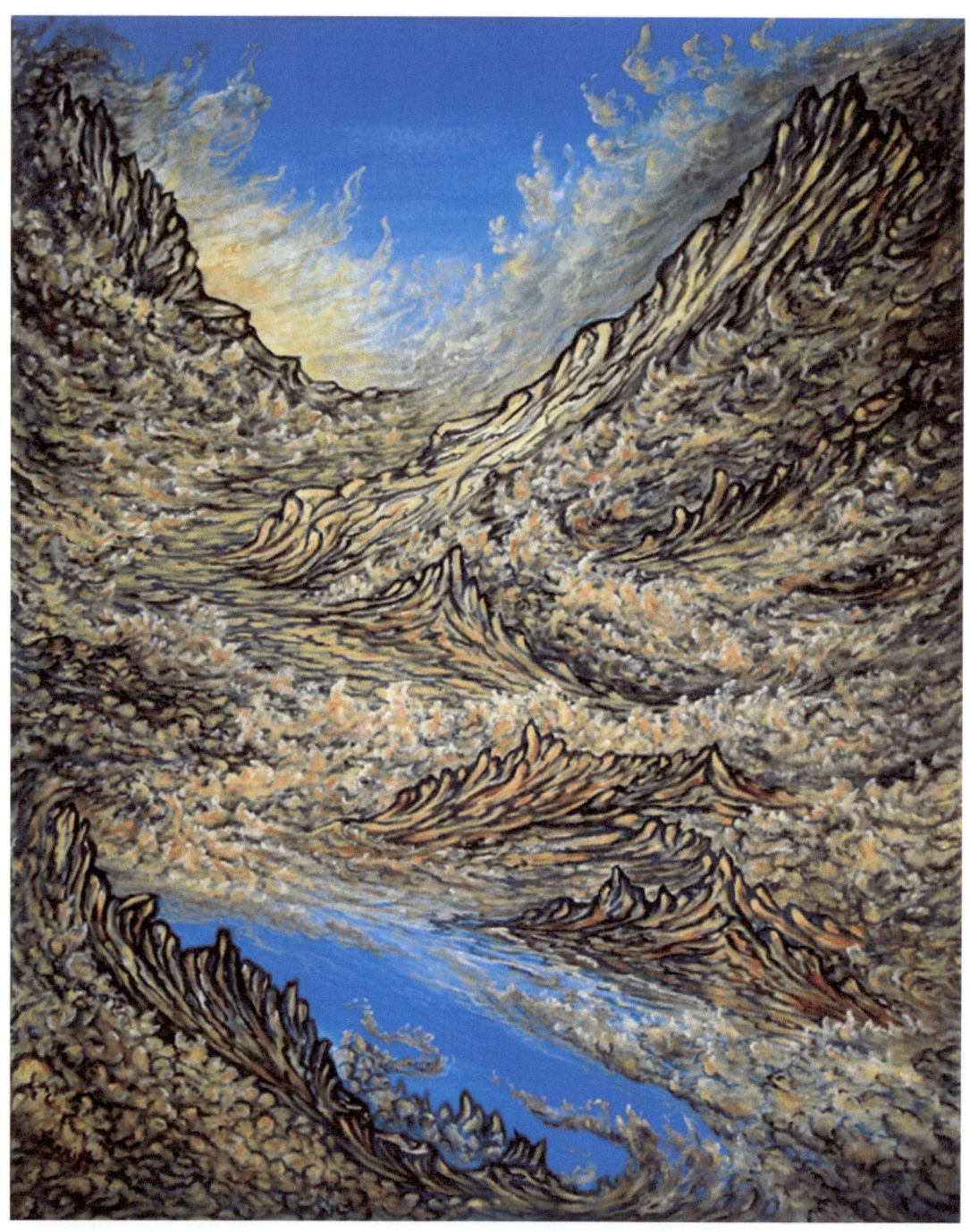

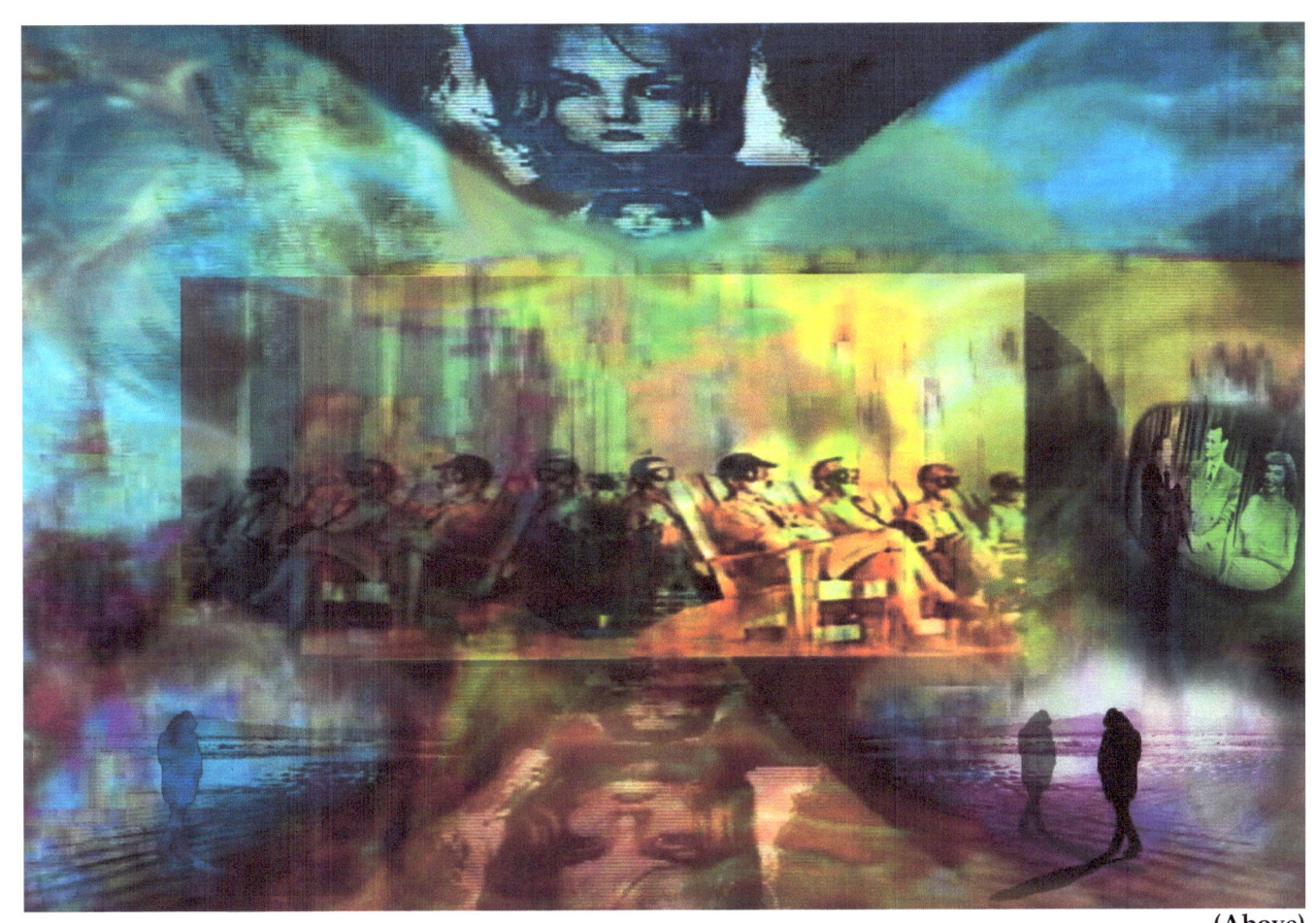

(Above)

12. Crossroads (Digital Image, 2010)

(Left)

11. Cloud Hidden   (Oil on Canvas, 24″ x 30″, 2009)

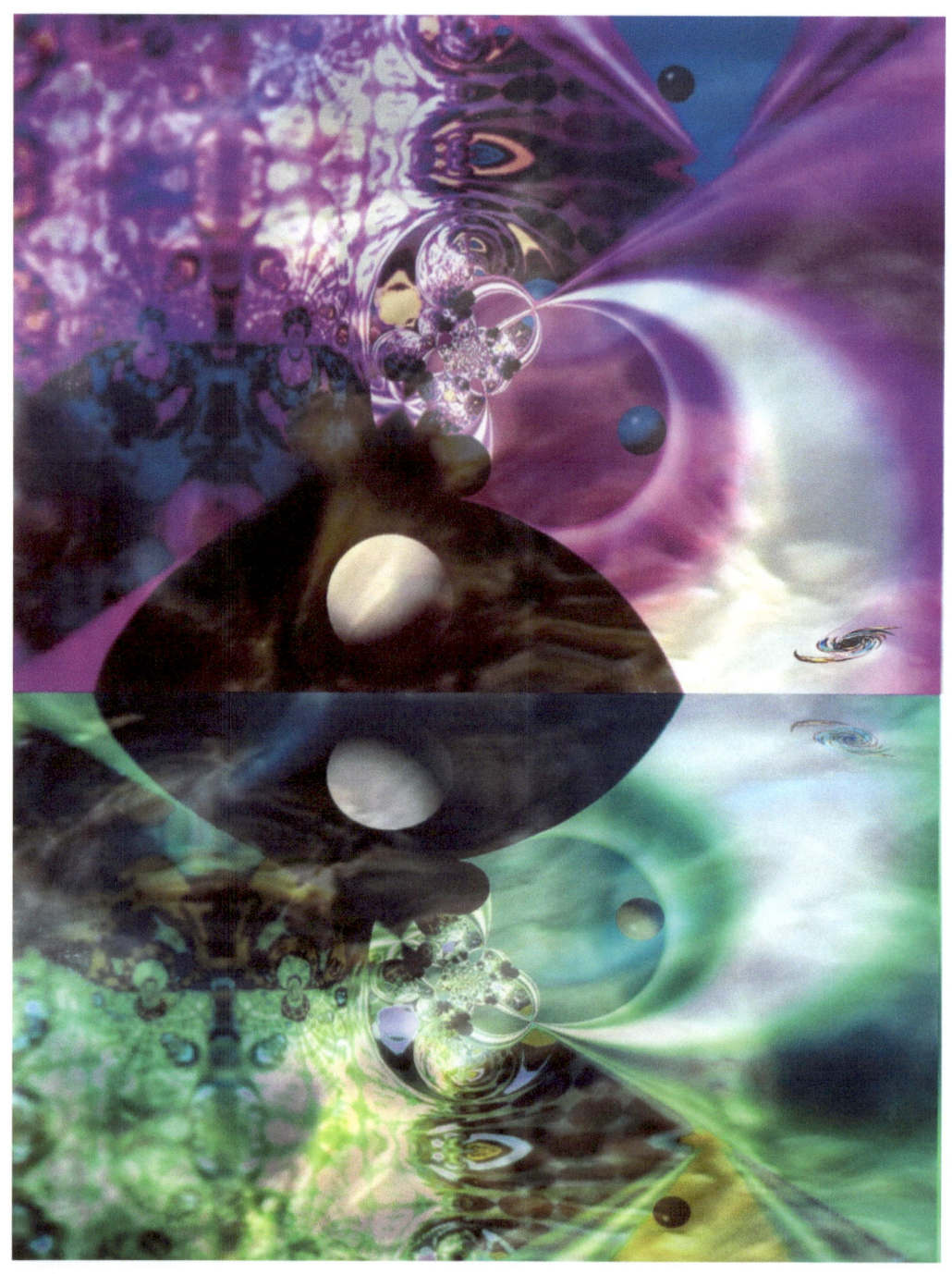

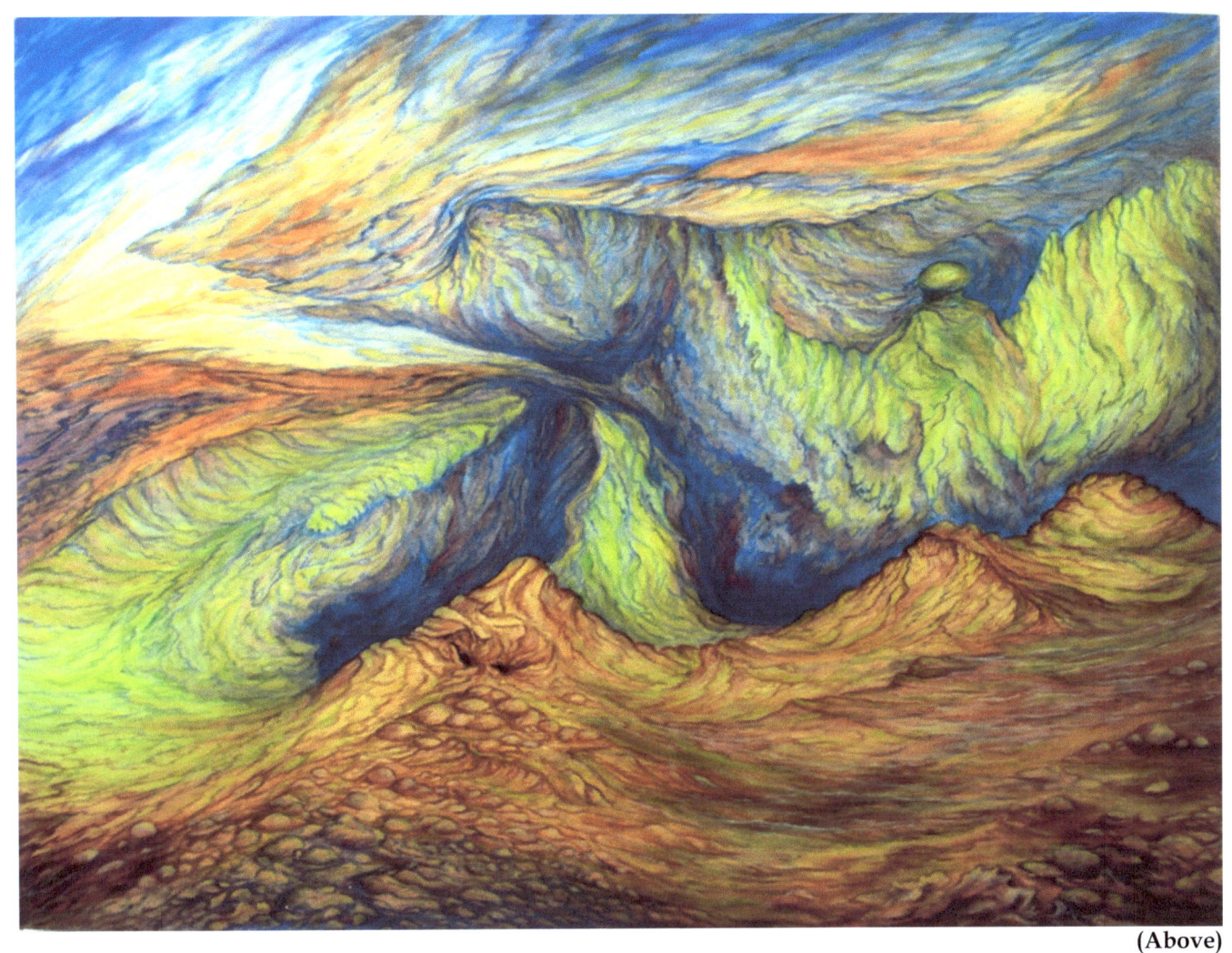

(Above)

14. Canyons (Oil on Canvas, 30" x 40", 2012)

(Left)

13. Magic Mirror (Digital Image, 2005)

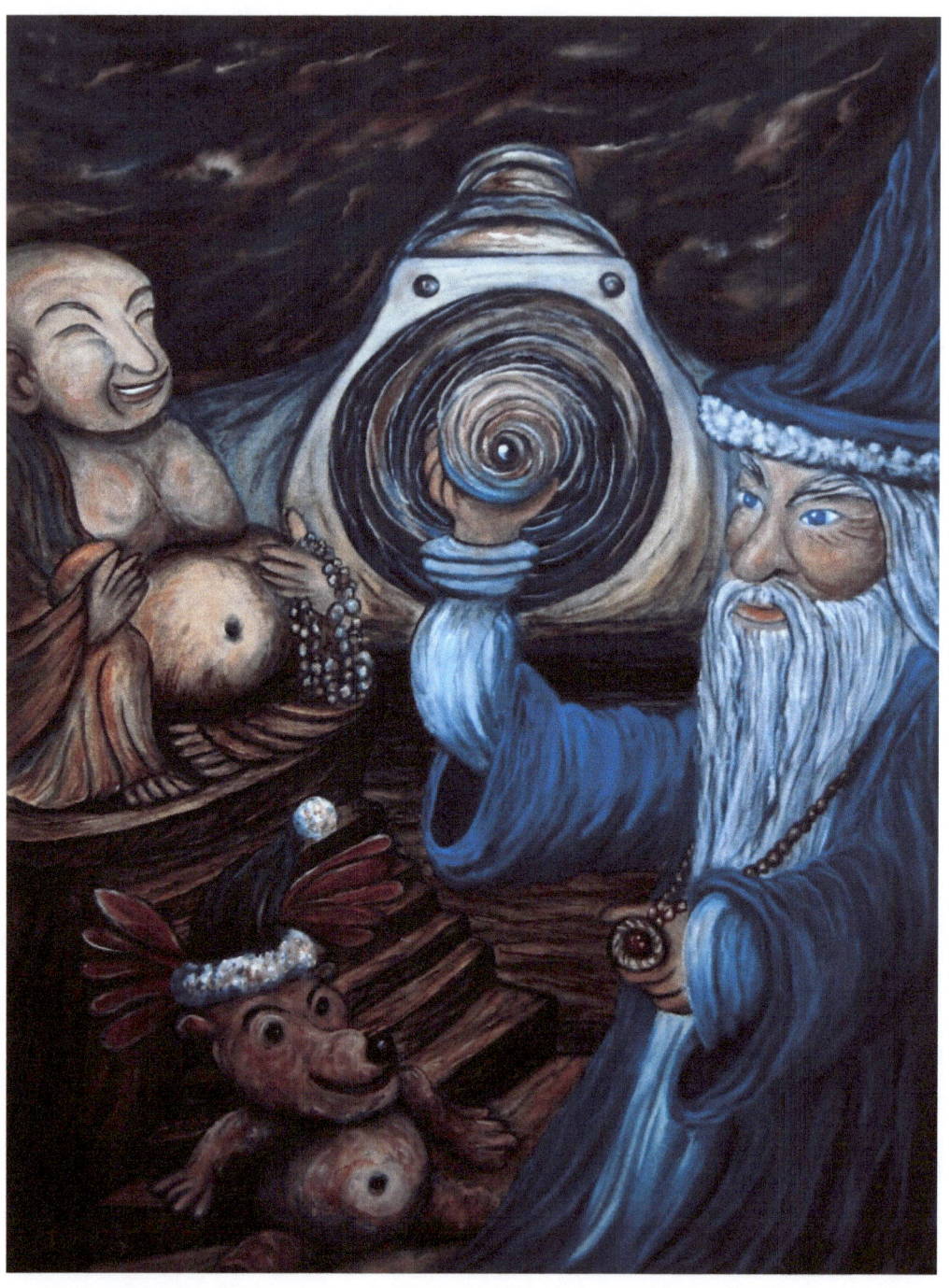

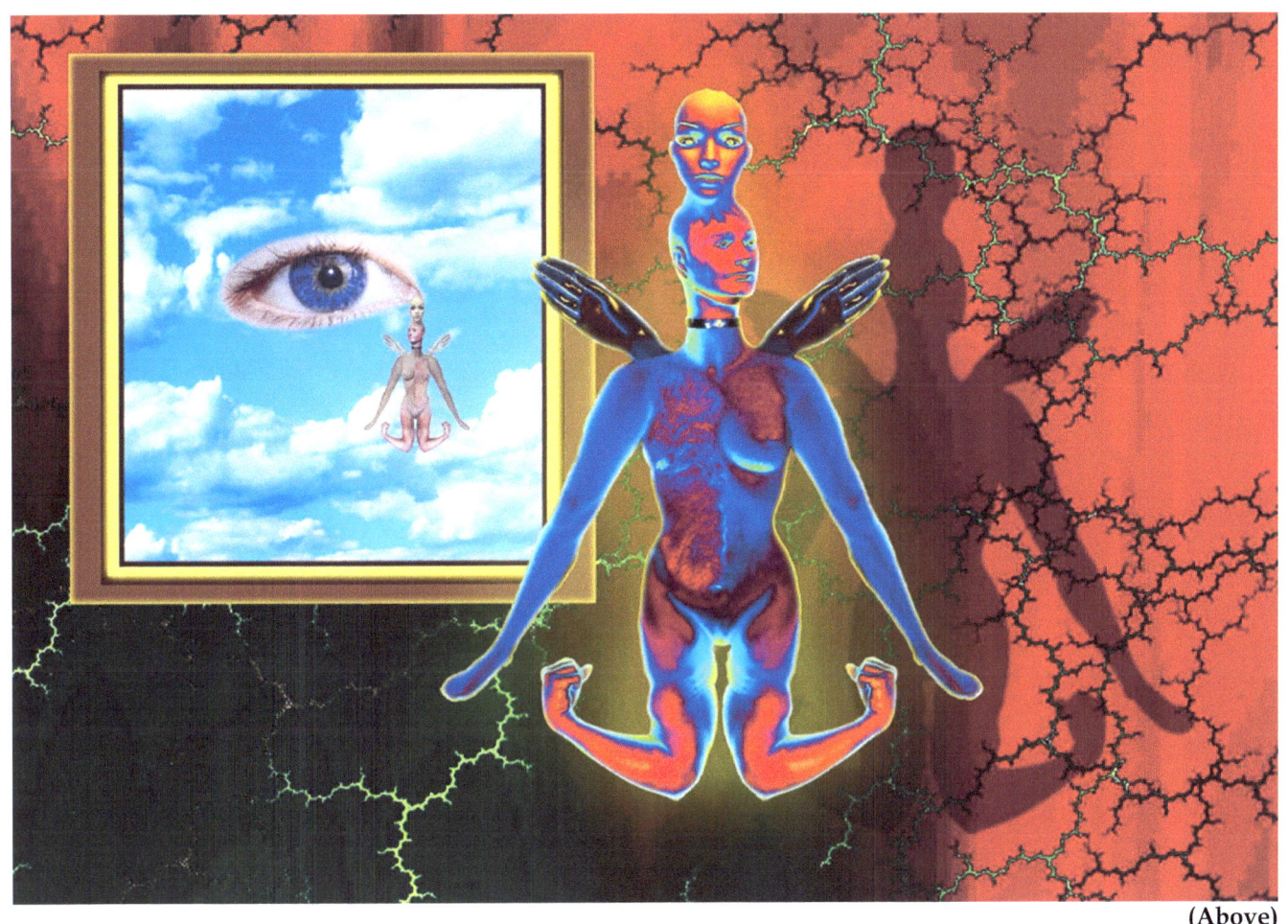

(Above)

16. Blue Eyed Dream (Digital Image, 2012)

(Left)

15. Oomphala (Oil on Canvas, 18″ x 24″, 2007)

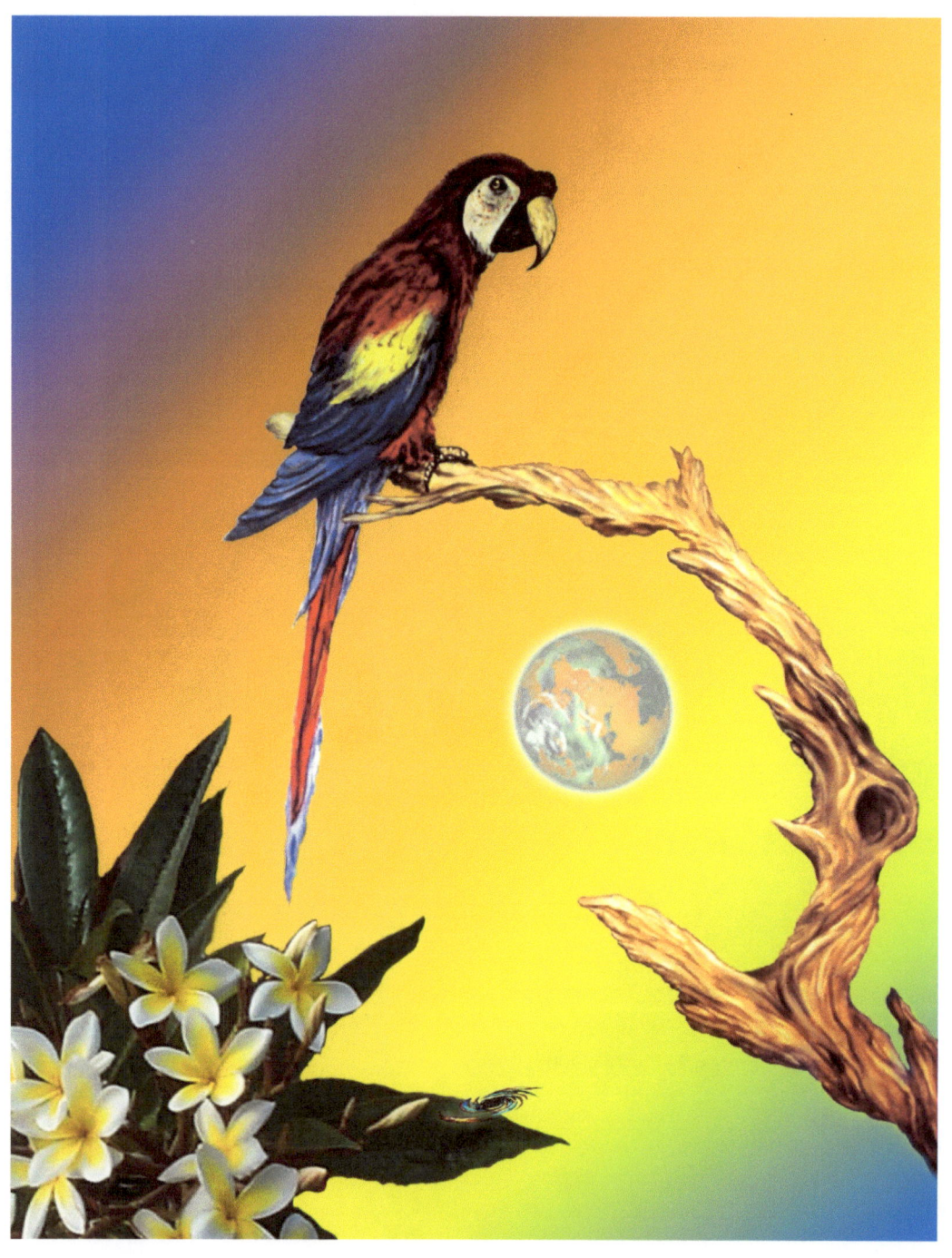

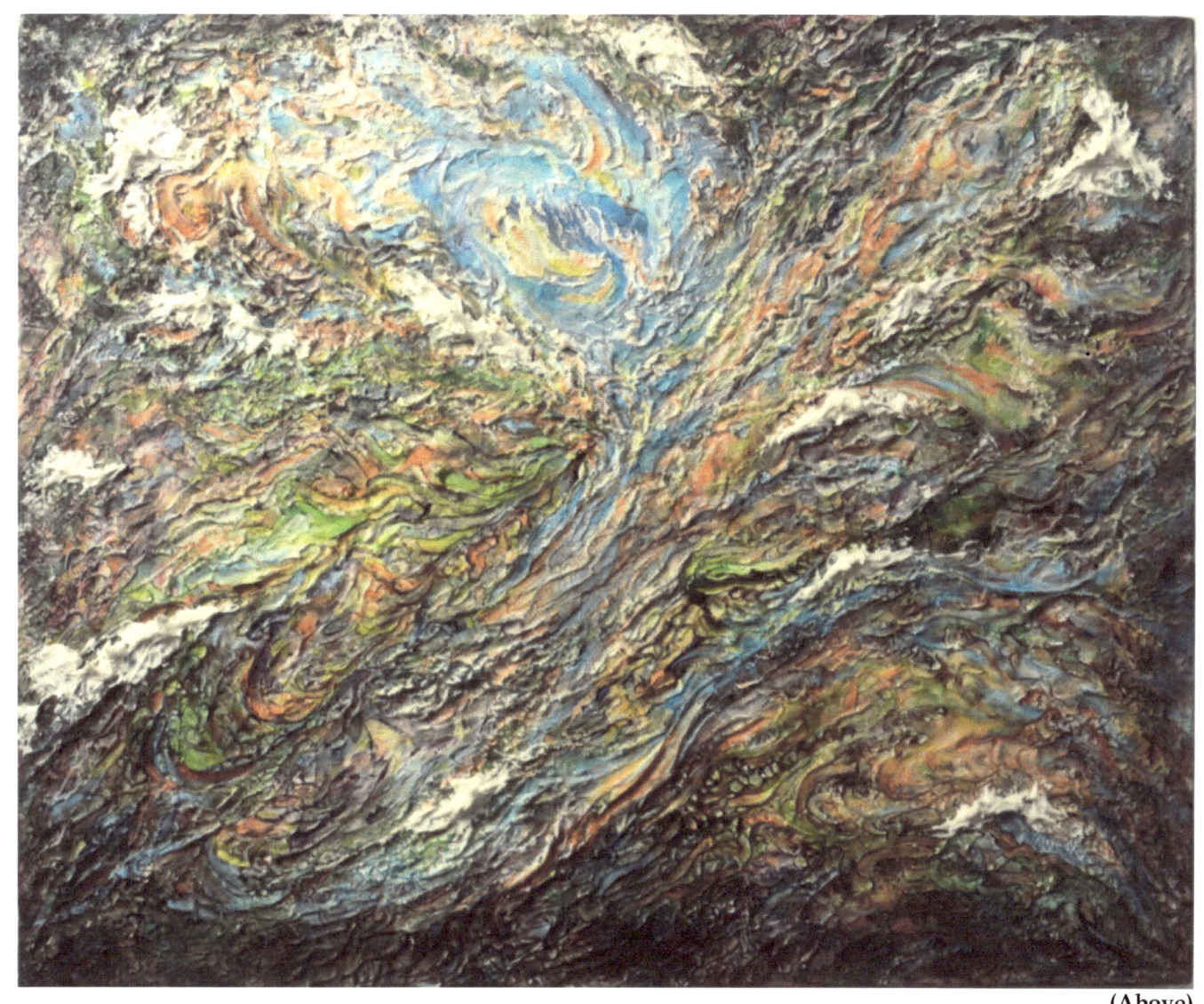

18. Higher Ground (Acrylic/Mixed Media on Canvas, 24″ x 30″, 2015)

(Left)

17. Lola Mae Bychu (Digital Image, 1999)

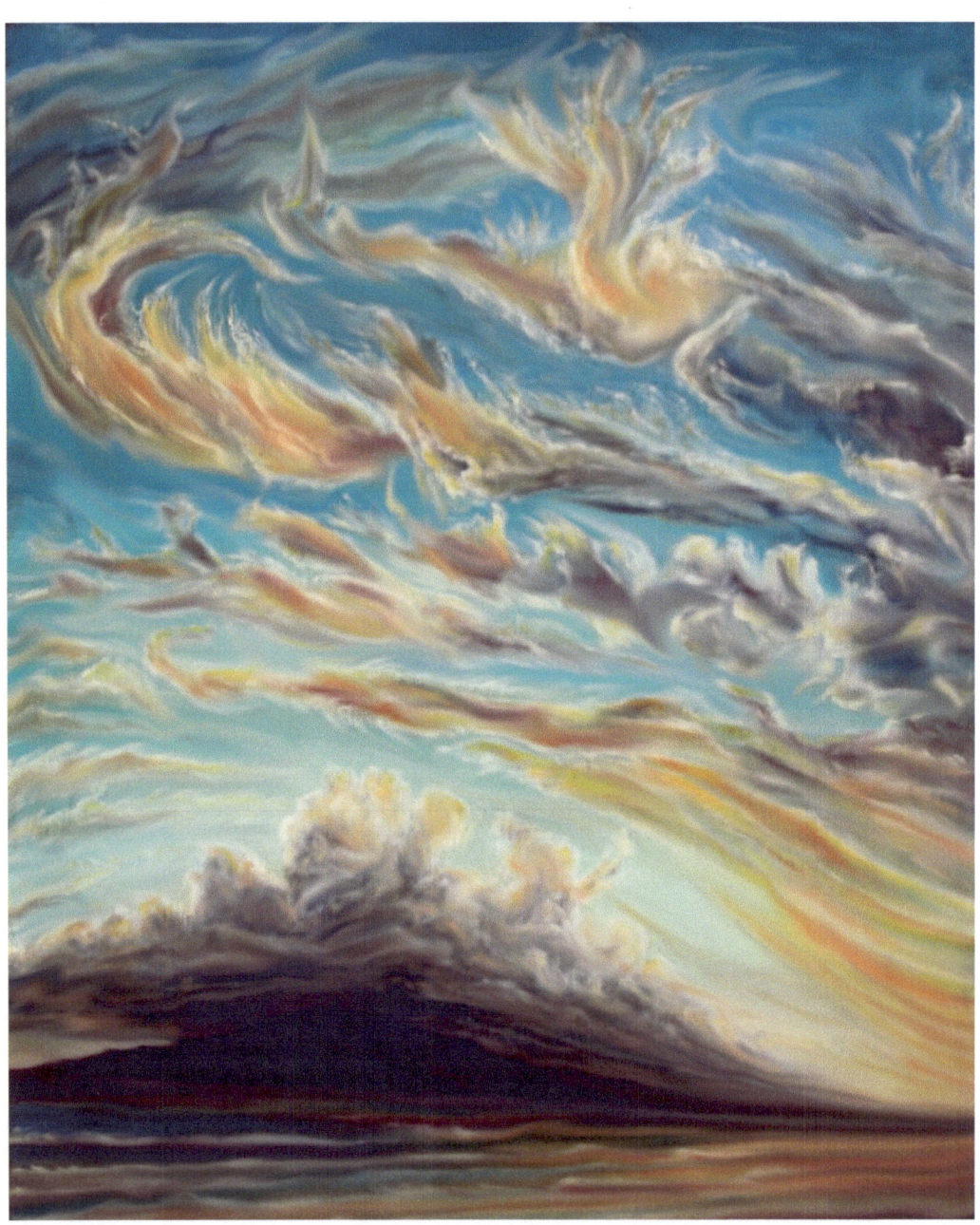

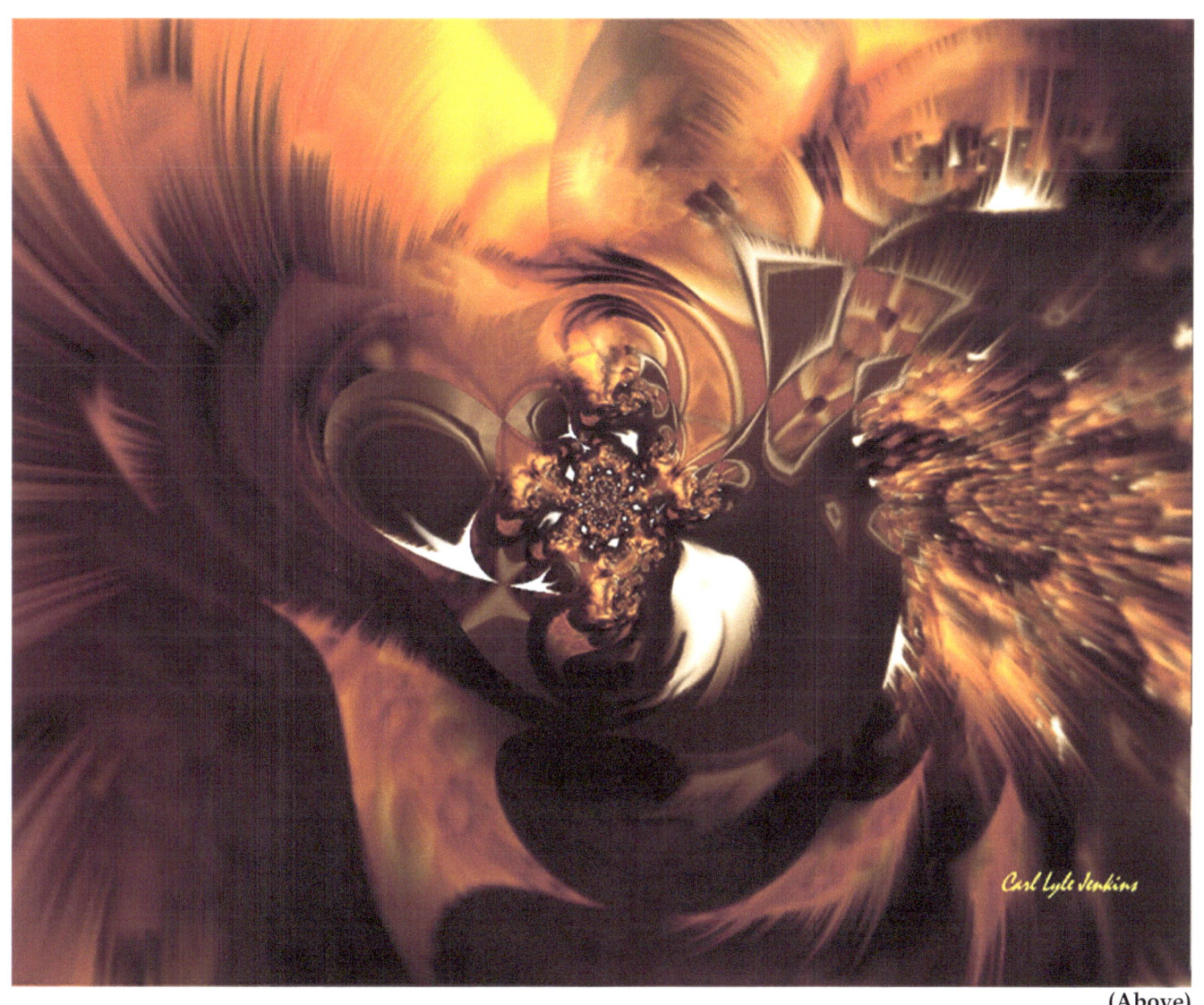

(Above)

20. *Feathered Fantasy* (Digital Image, 2000)

(Left)

19. *Lanai* (Oil on Canvas, 18″ x 24″, 1998)

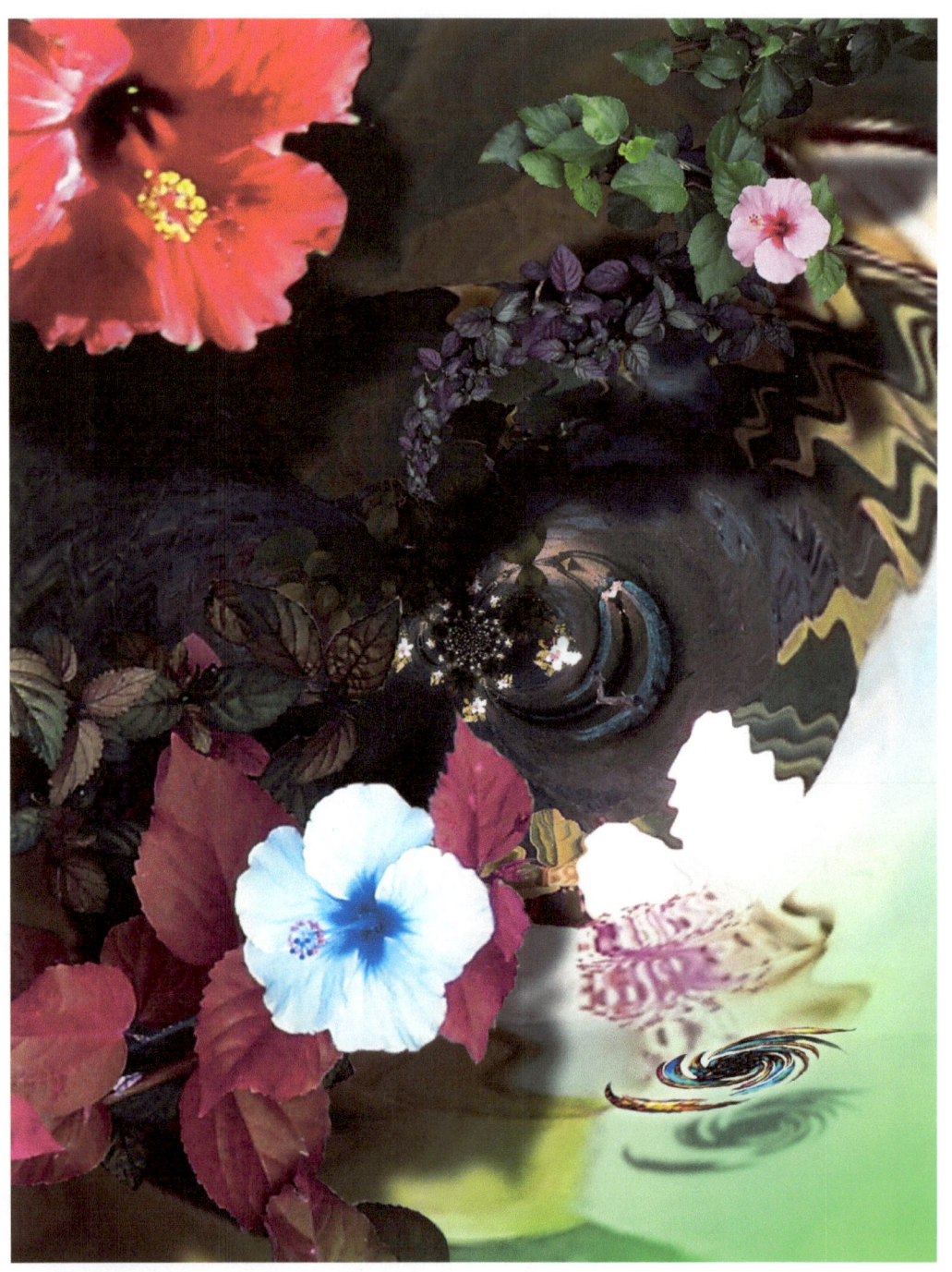

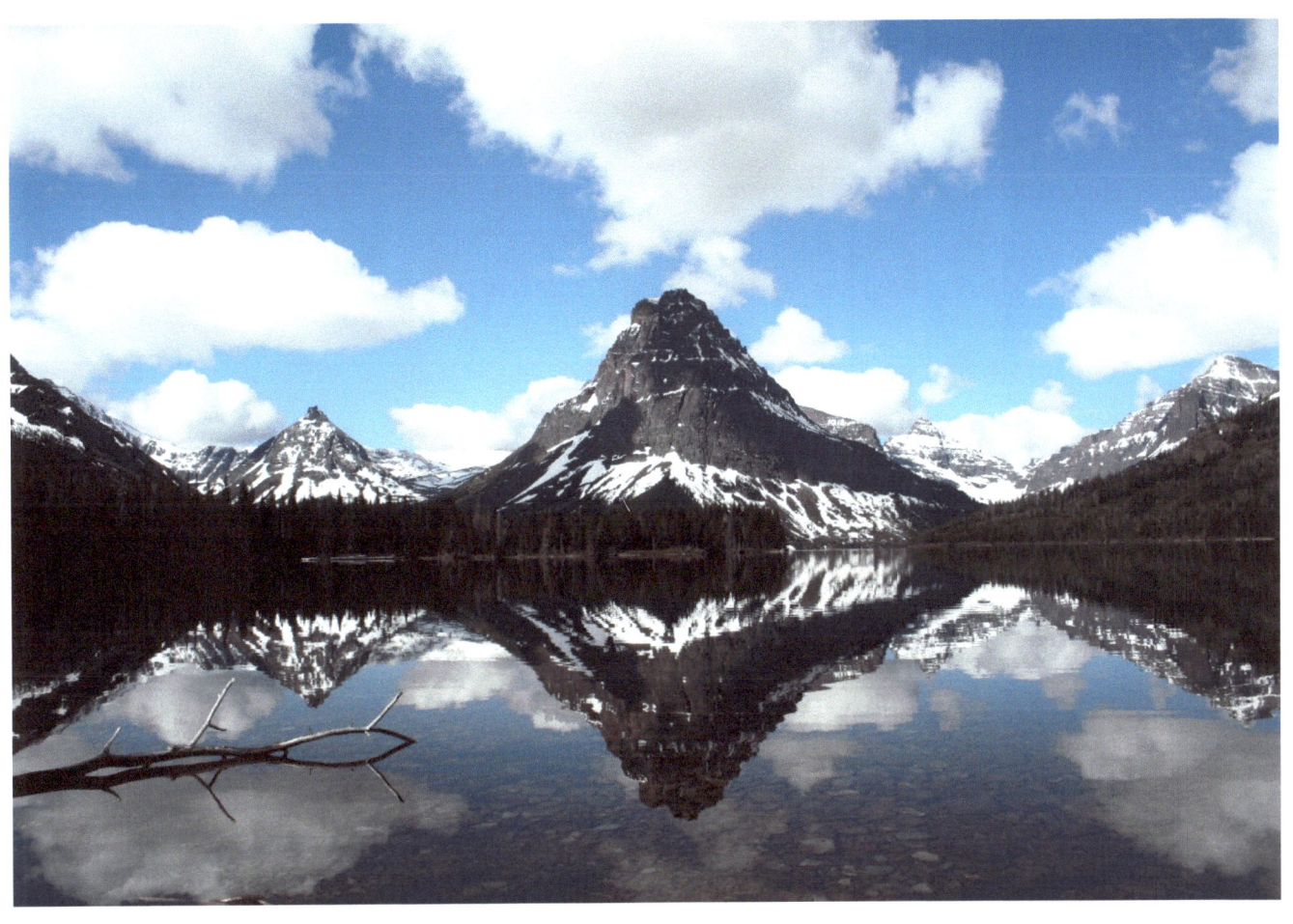

22. *Spring, Two Medicine Lake, Glacier National Park, USA* (Photo, 2007)

21. *Fluertex* (Digital Image, 2005)

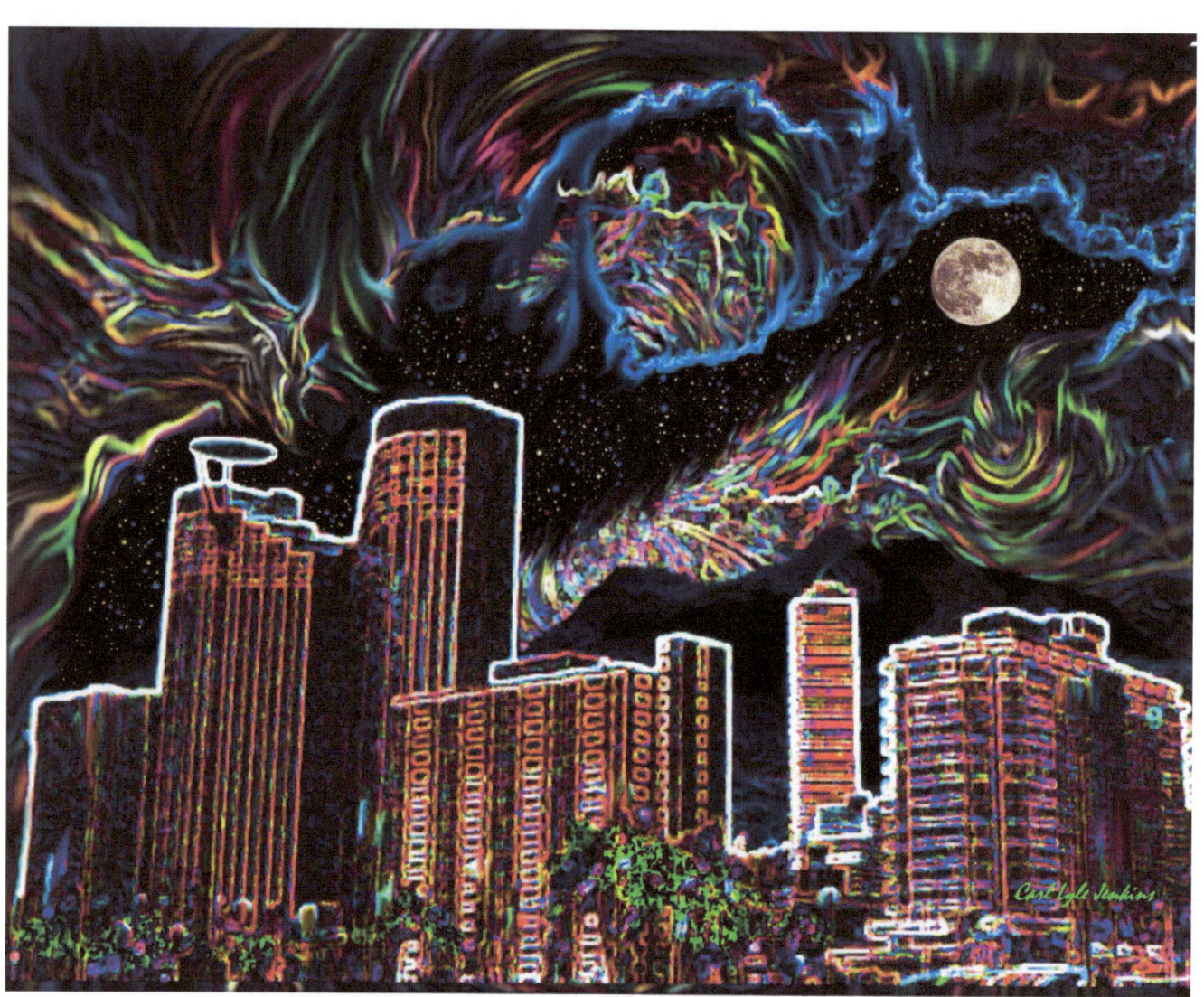

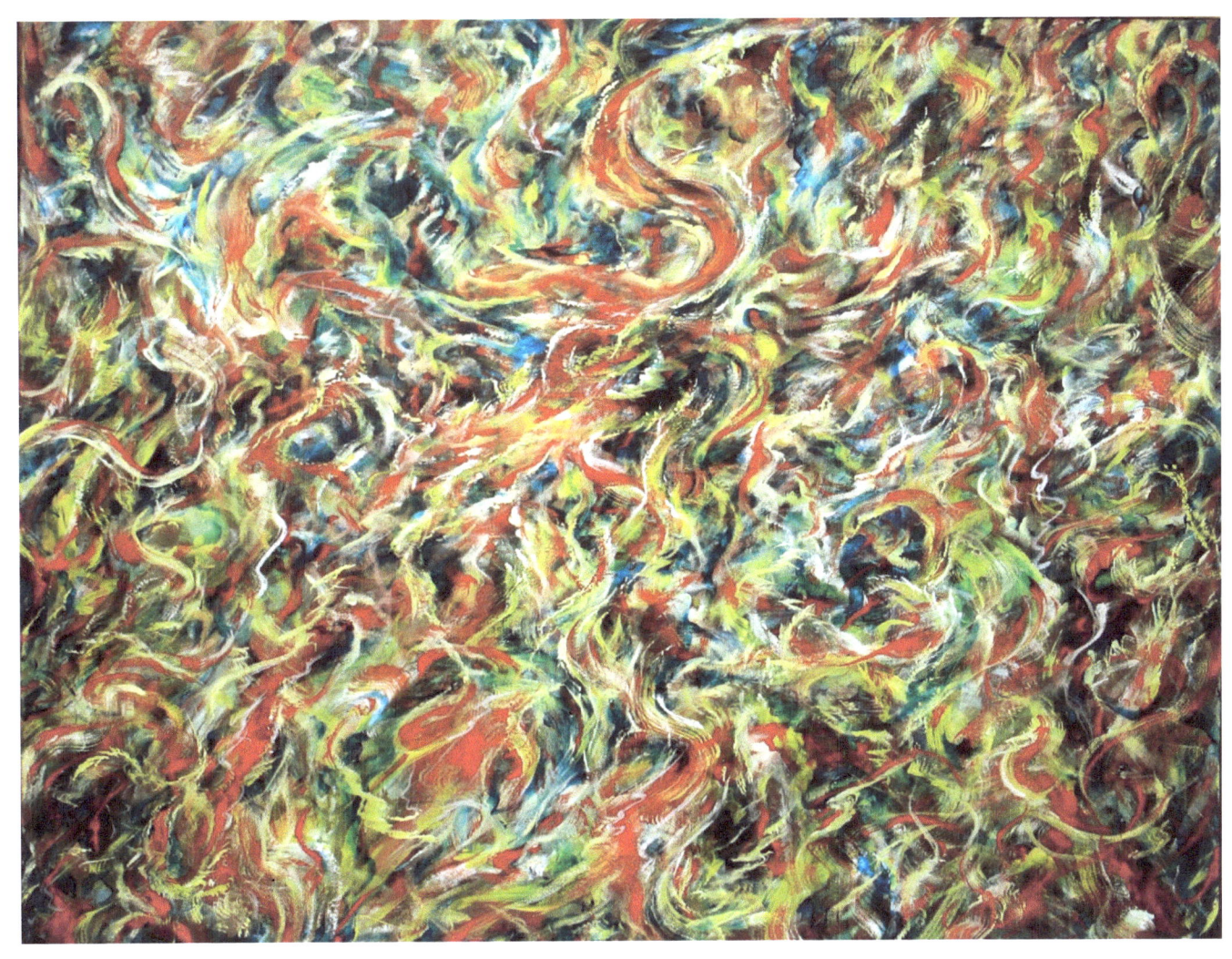

(Above)

24. Firedance (Acrylic Painting on Canvas, 36″ x 48″, 2012)

(Left)

23. Oahu Huhu (Digital Image, 2002)

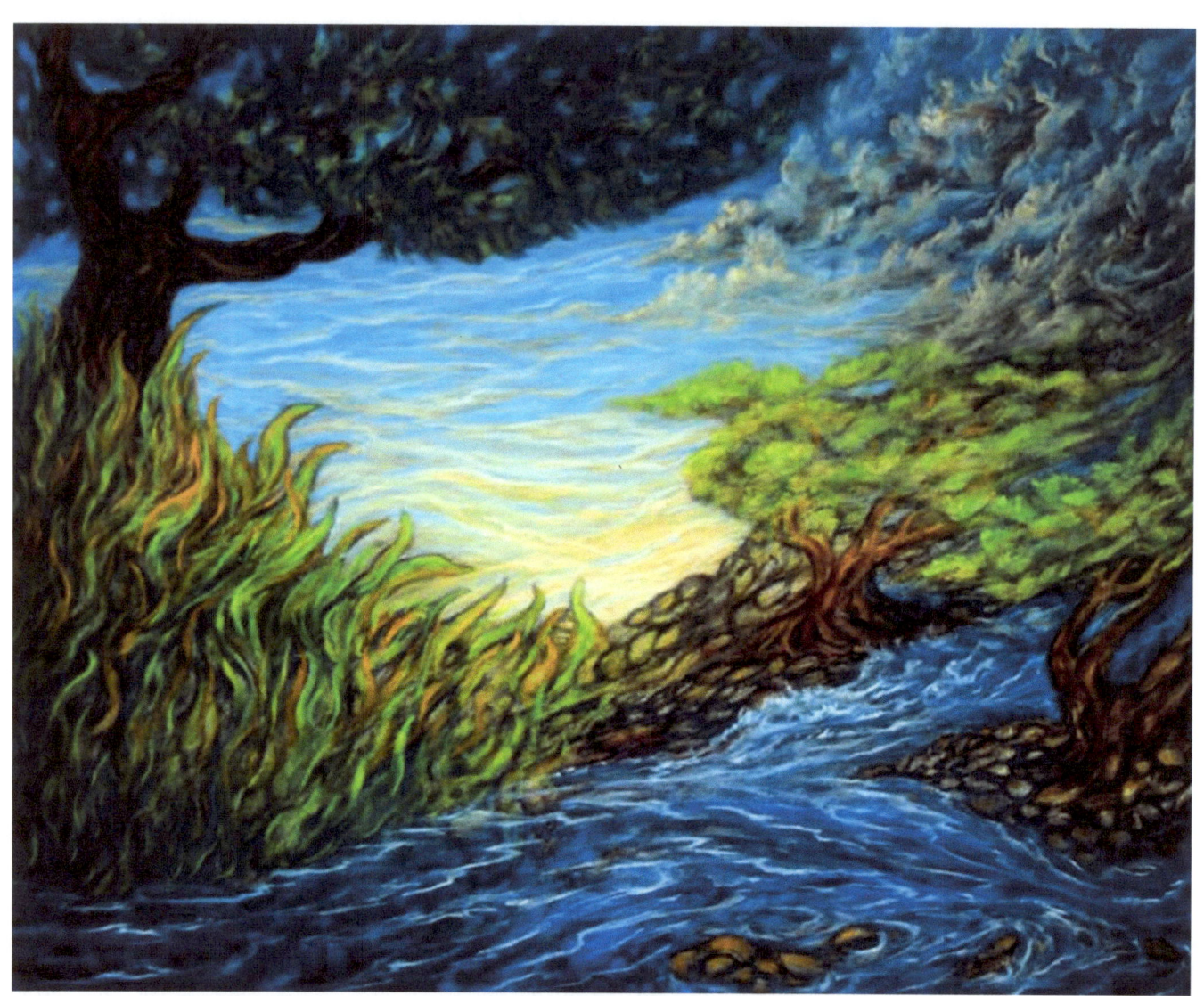

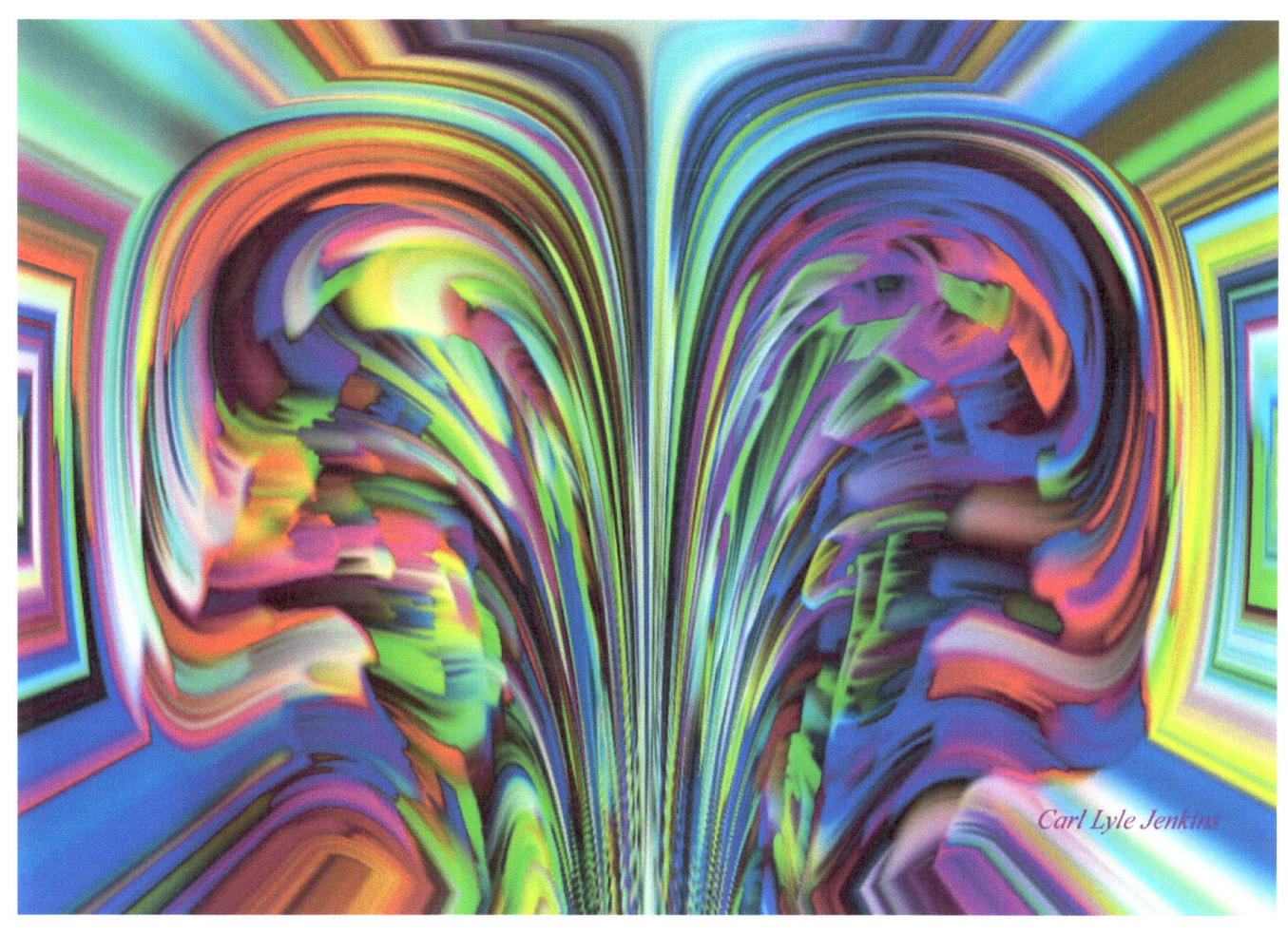

Carl Lyle Jenkins

(Above)
26. *Janus* (Digital Image, 2012)

(Left)
25. *The River* (Oil on Canvas, 24″ x 30″, 2012)

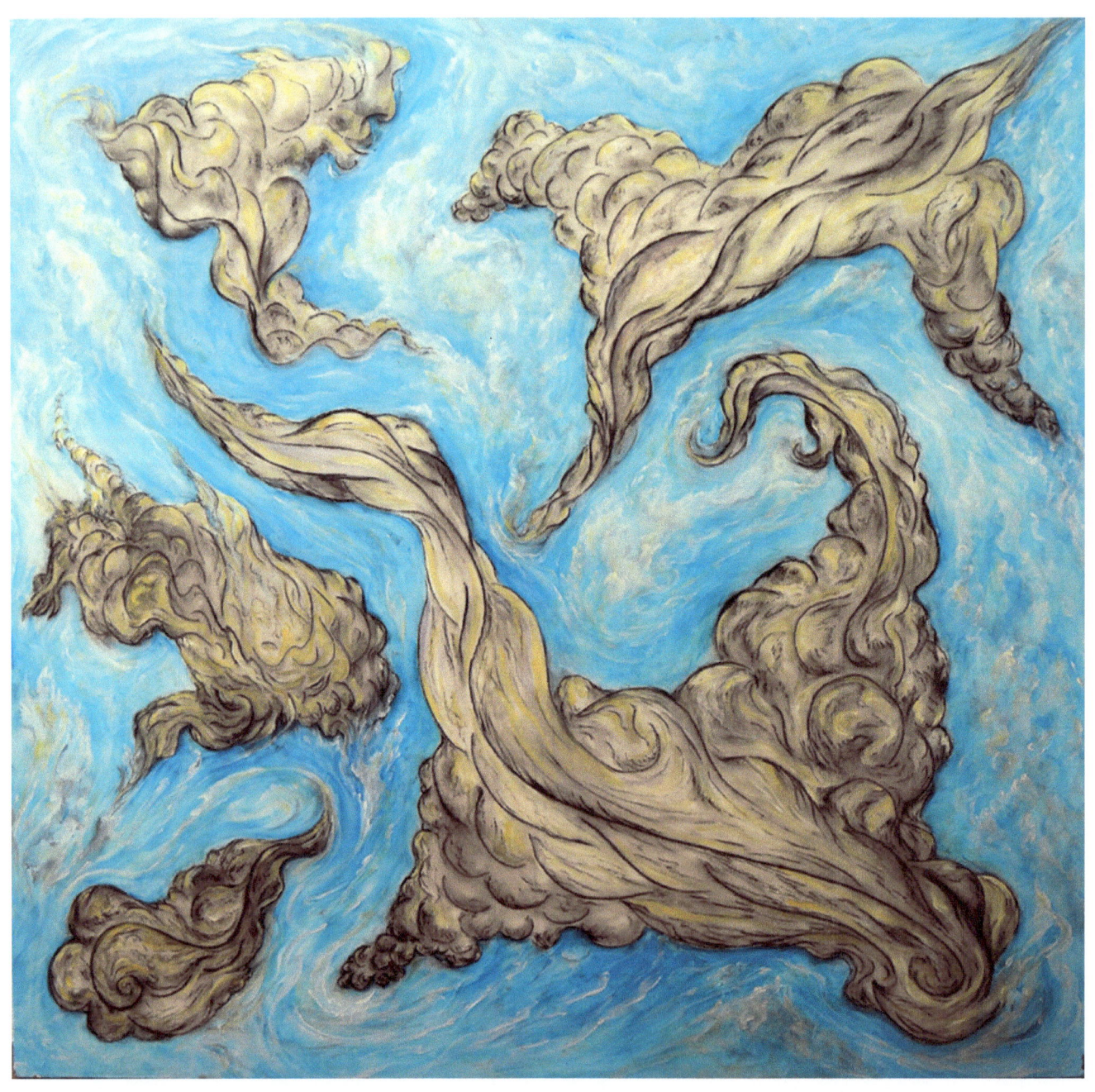

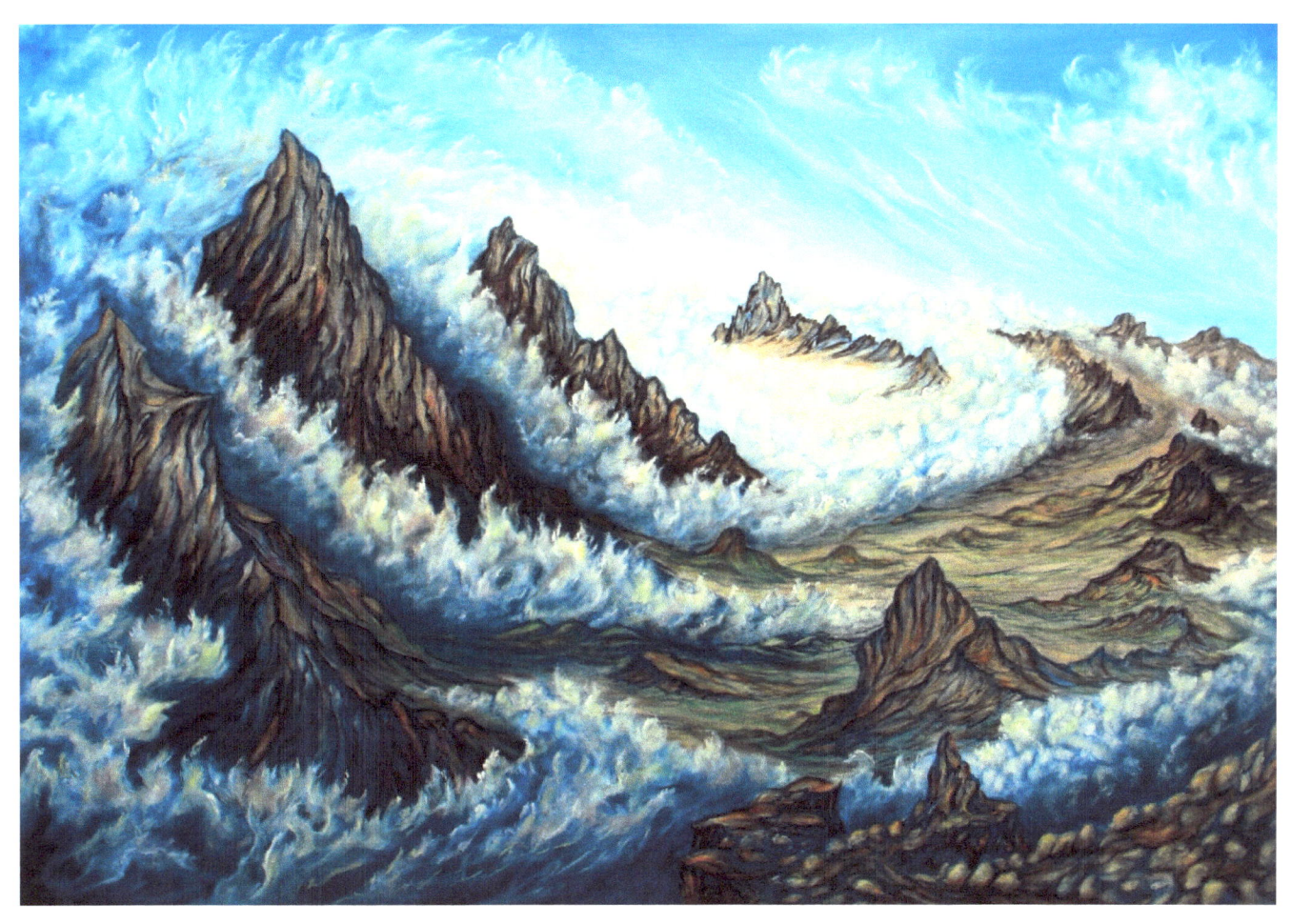

(Above)

28. Vista (Oil on Canvas, 24″ x 36″, 2012)

(Left)

27. Out of the Blue (Acrylic Painting on Masonite, 48″ x 48″, 2015)

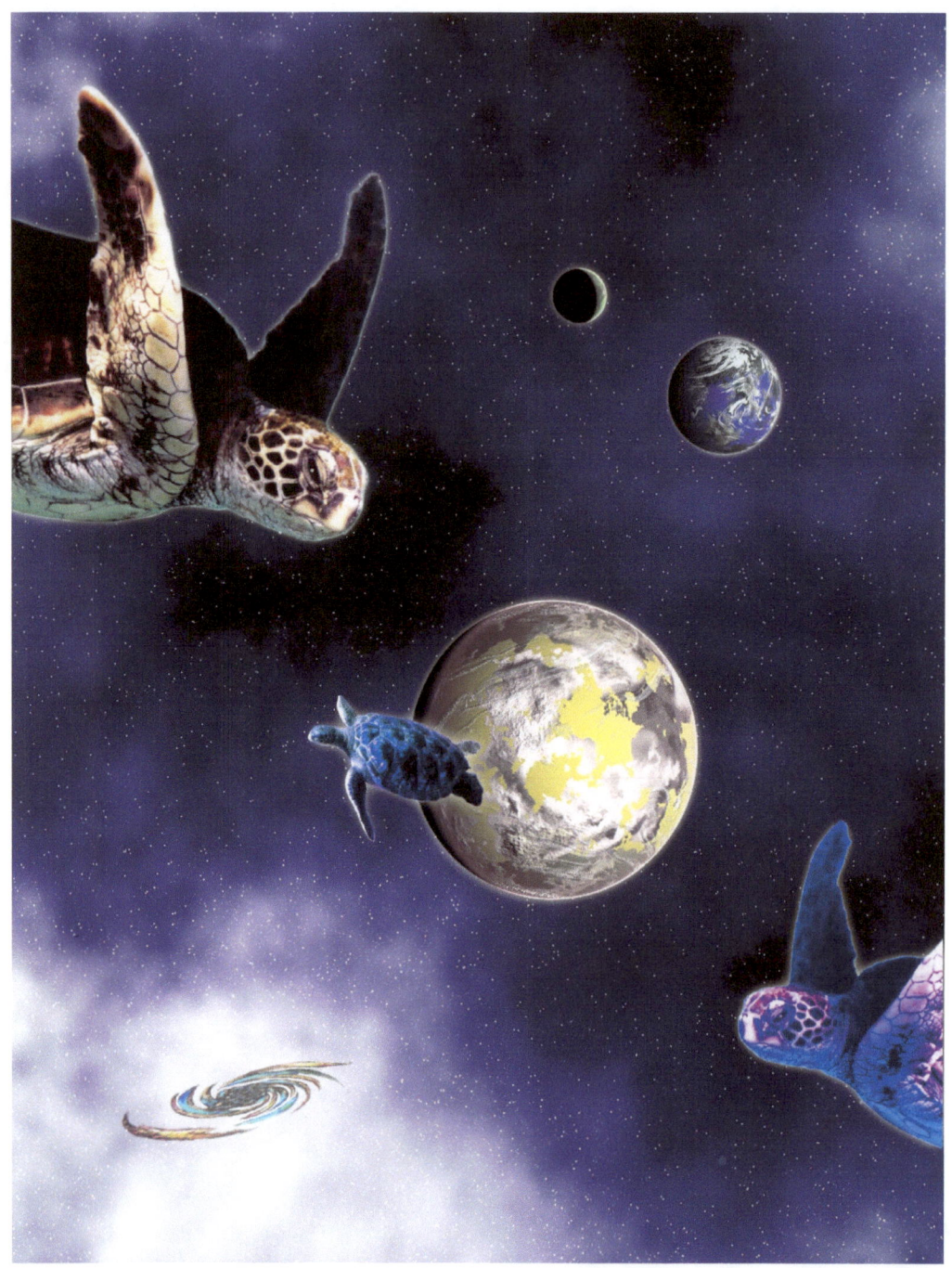

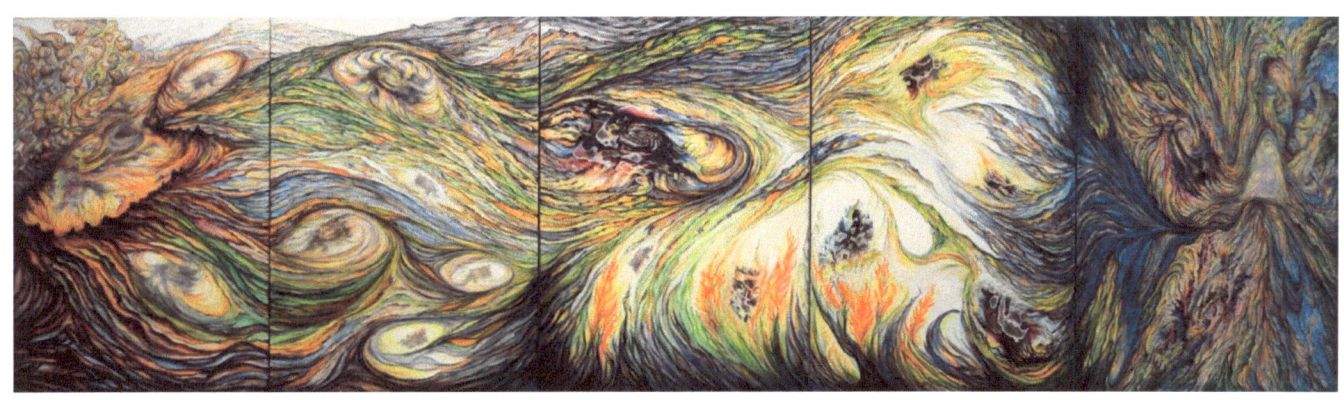

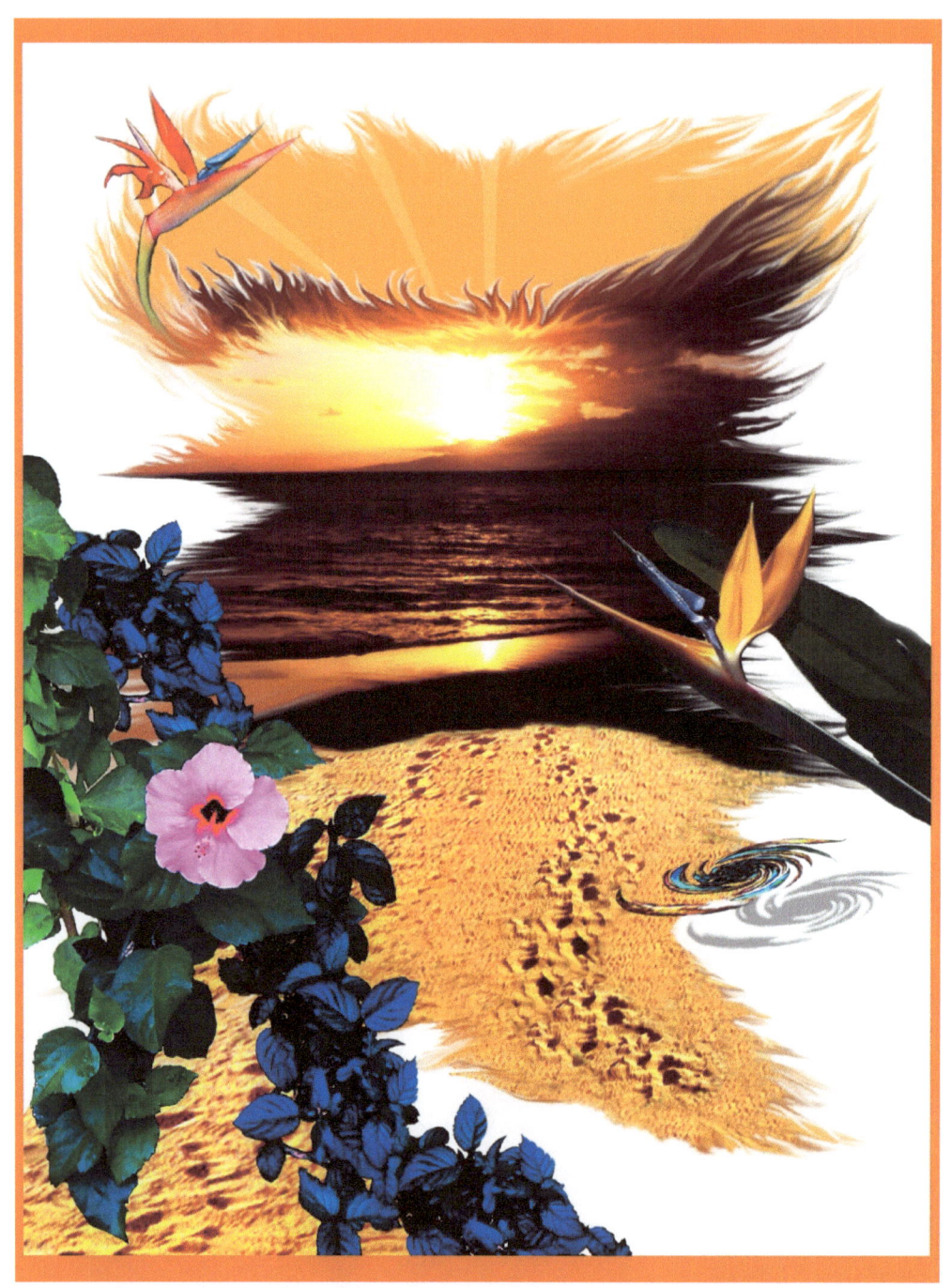

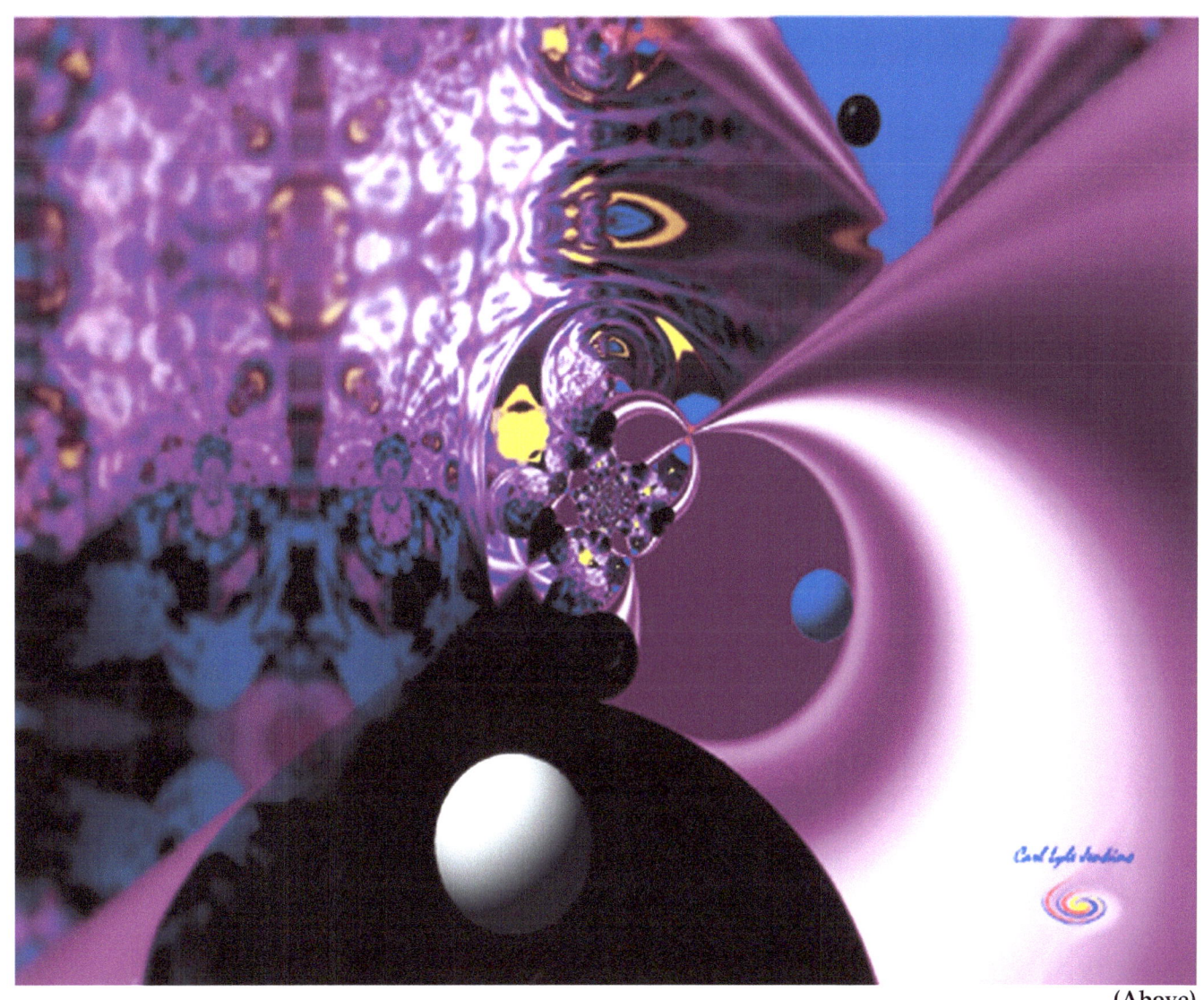

(Above)

32. *The Visitation* (Digital Image, 1999)

(Left)

31. *Paradise Point* (Digital Image, 2001

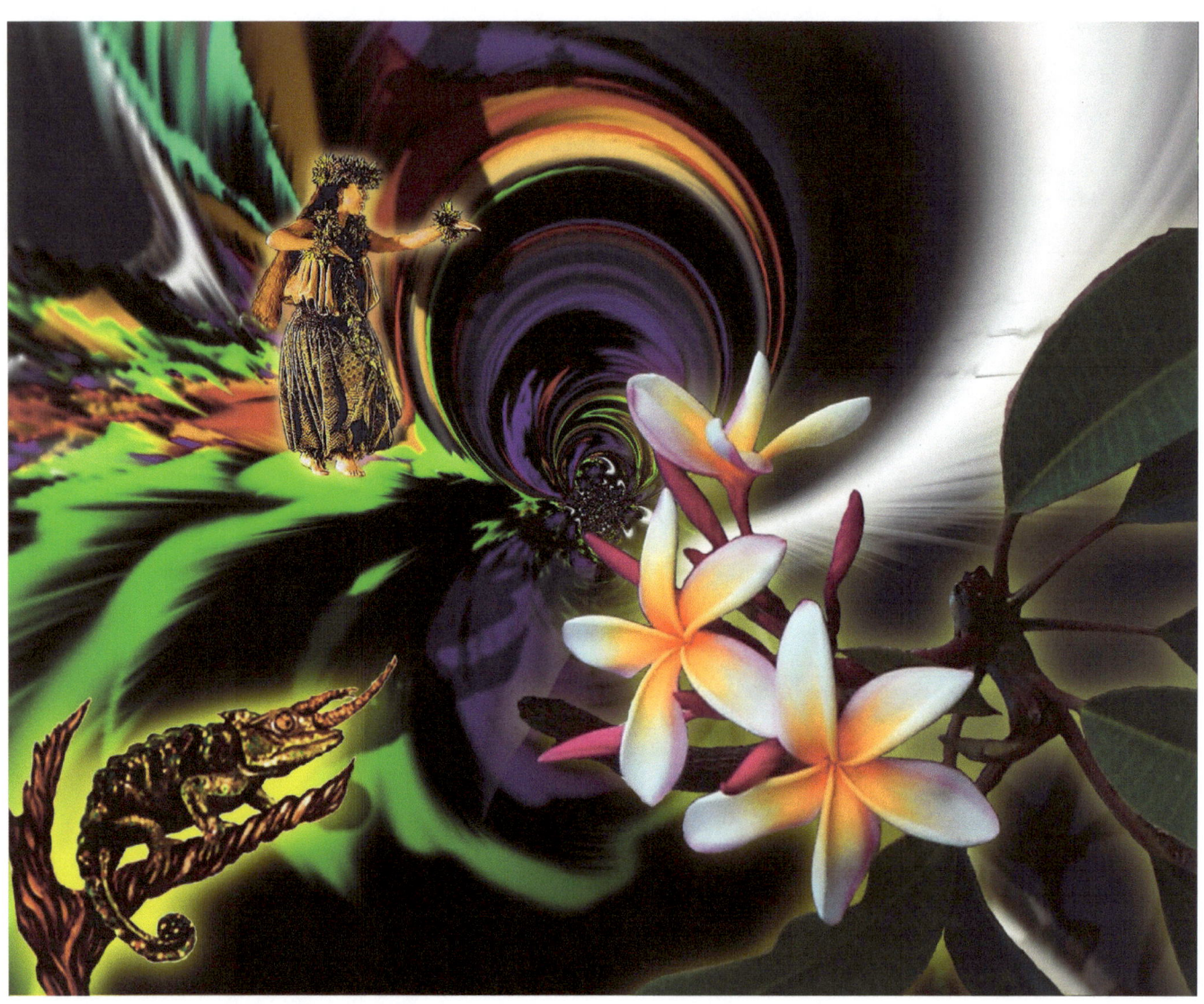

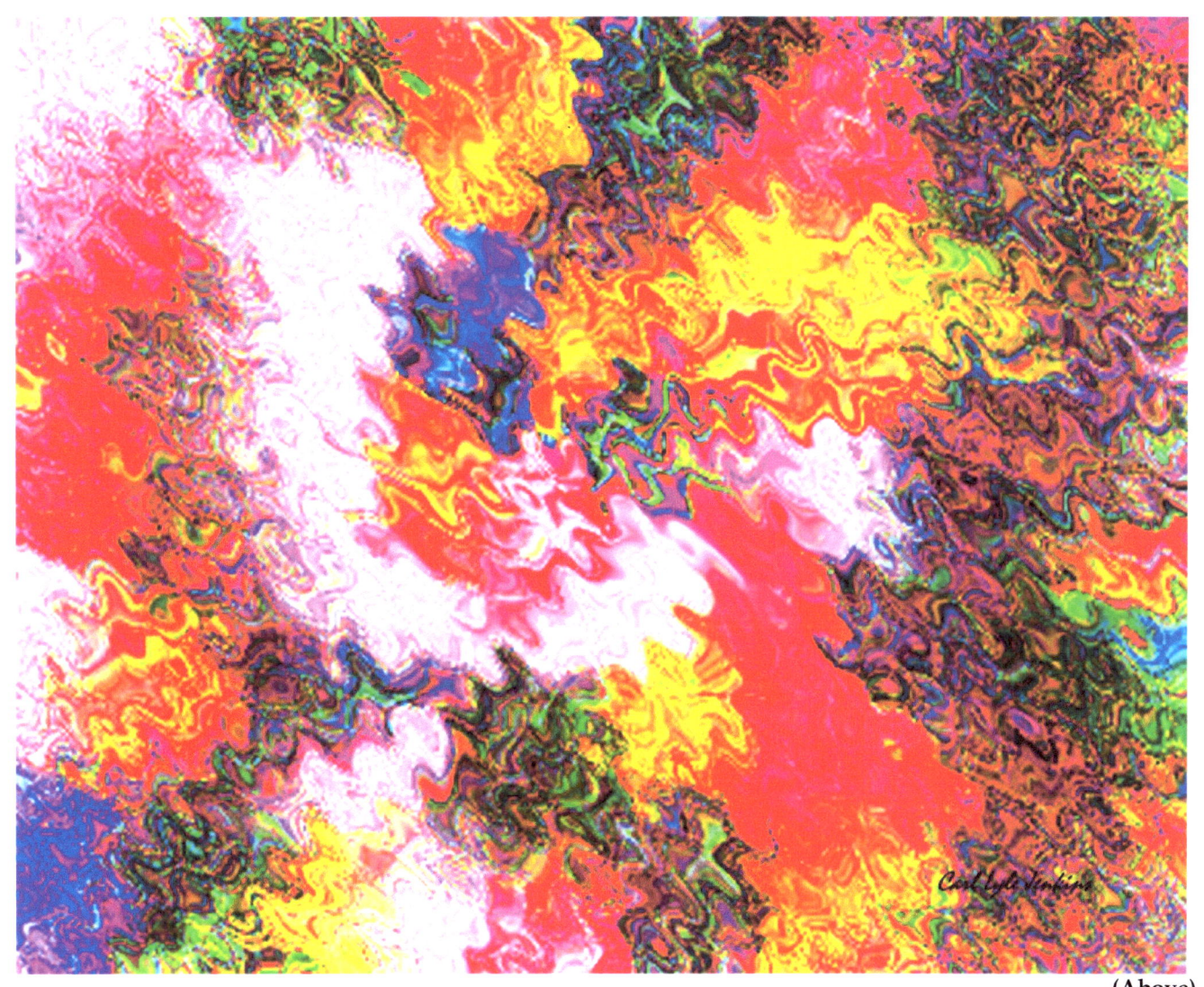

(Above)

34. Flamenco (Digital Image, 2002)

(Left)

33. Dancing with Destiny (Digital Image, 2002)

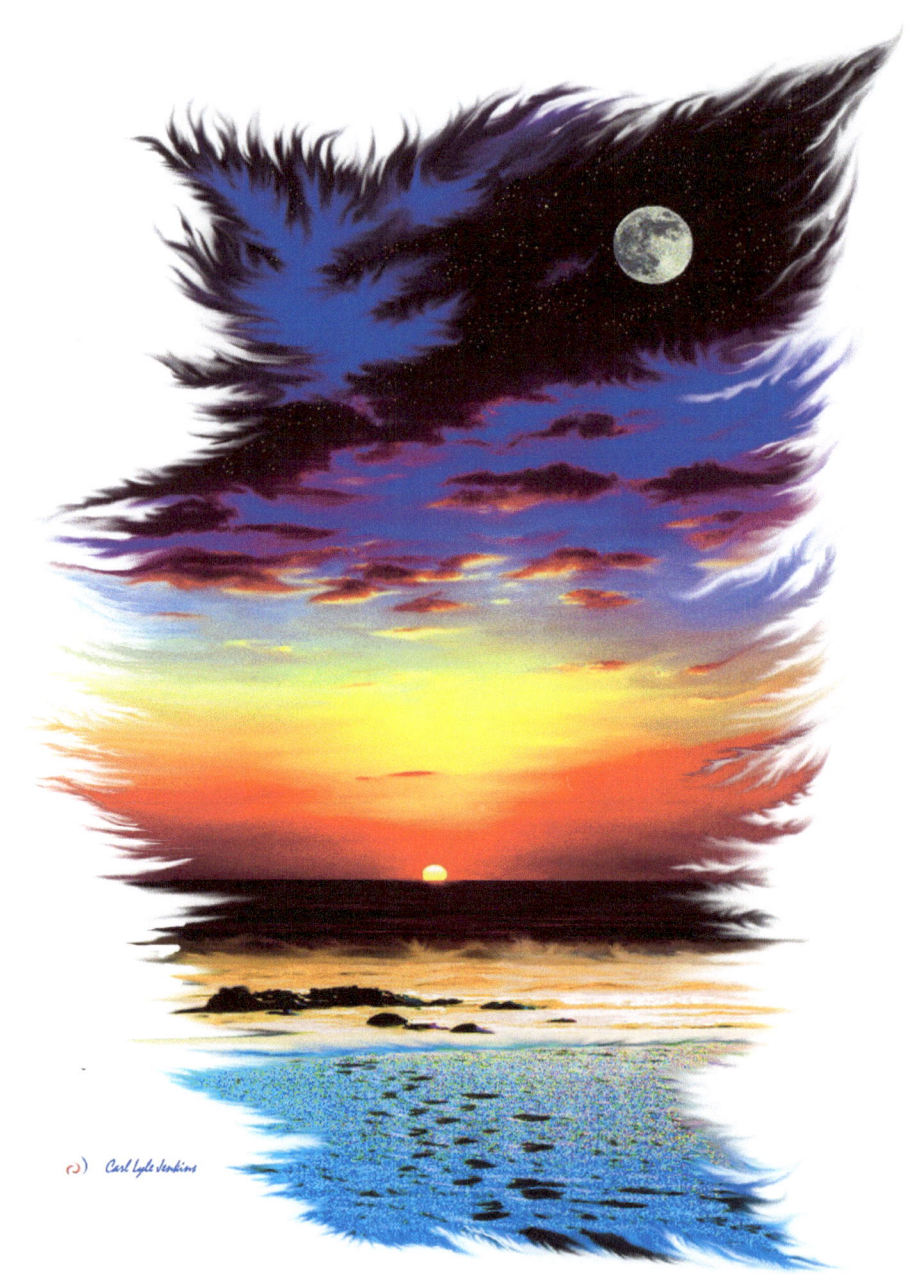

Carl Lyle Jenkins

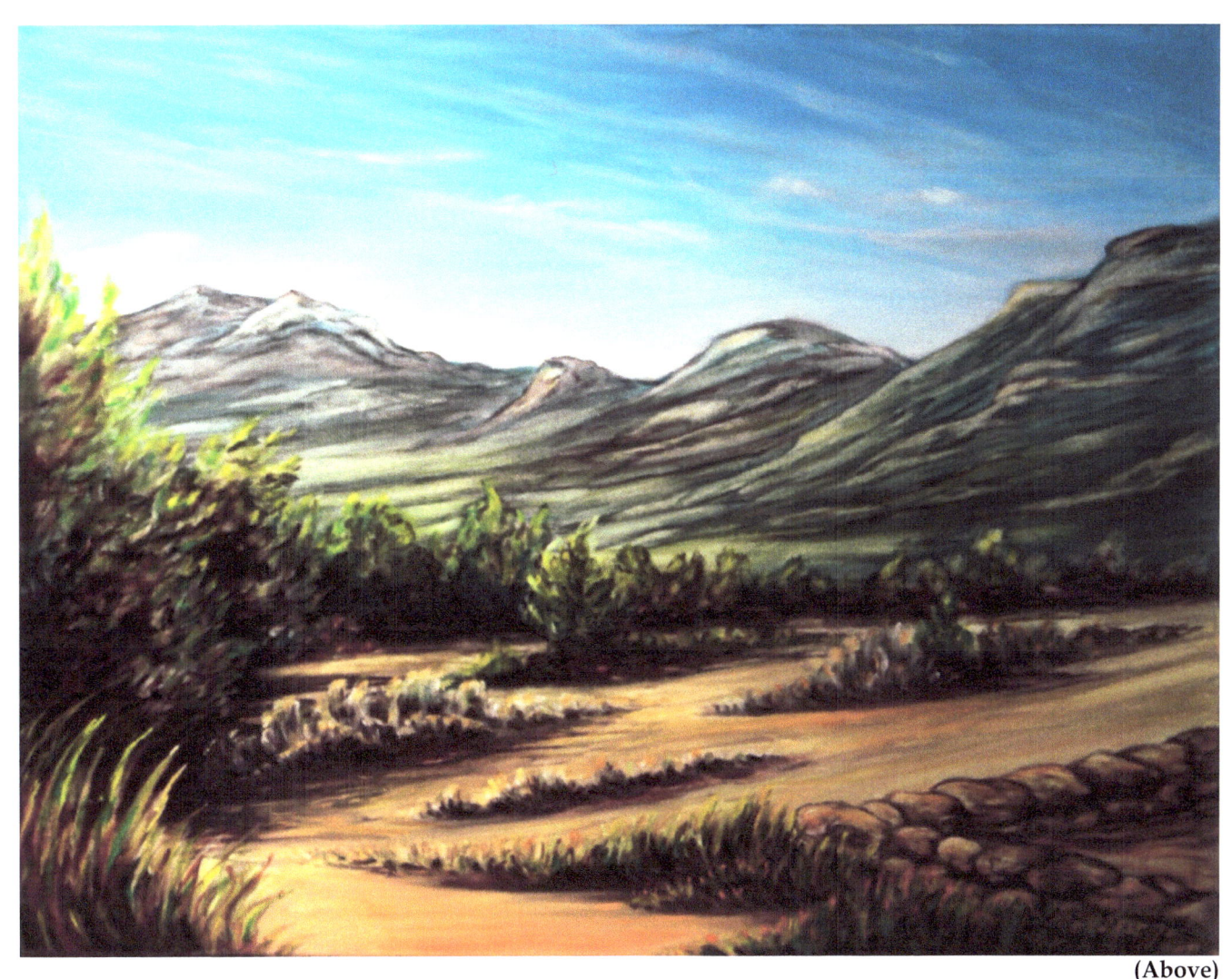

(Above)

36. Pecos Ruins (Oil on Canvas, 18″ x 24″, 2008)

(Left)

35. Secret Beach (Digital Image, 2001)

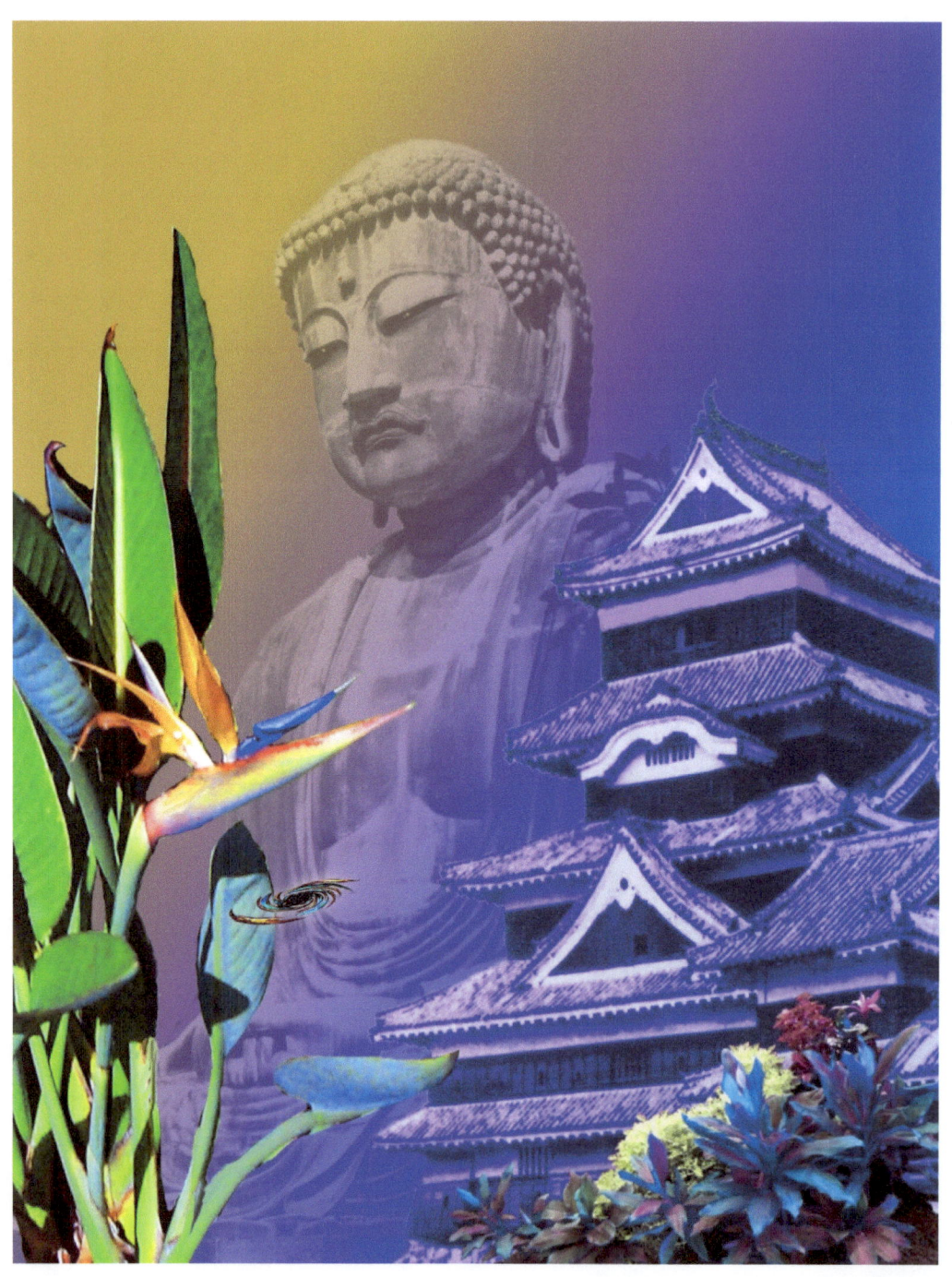

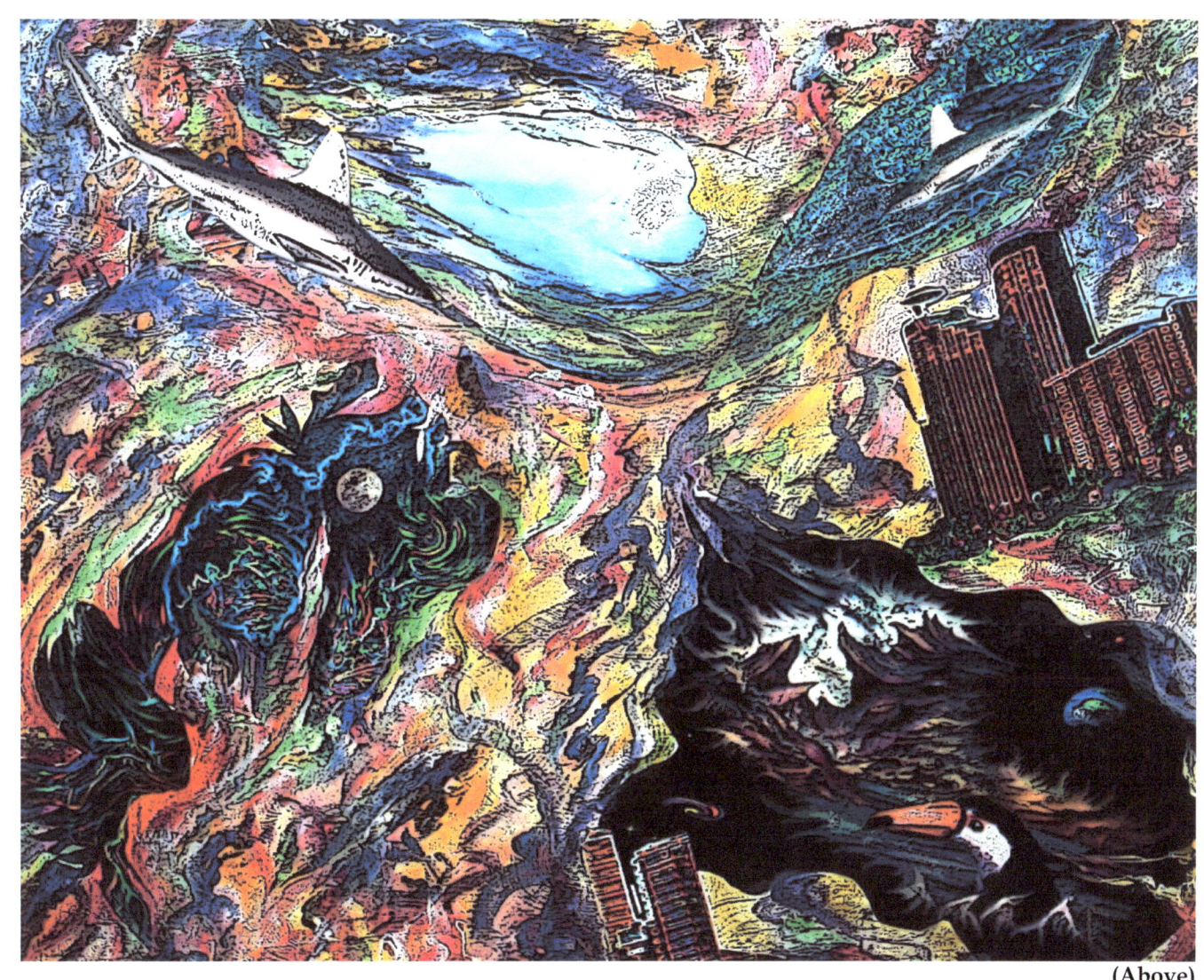

(Above)

38. Cloudy with a Chance of Sharks (Digital Image, 2014)

(Left)

37. Nirvana (Digital Image, 2004)

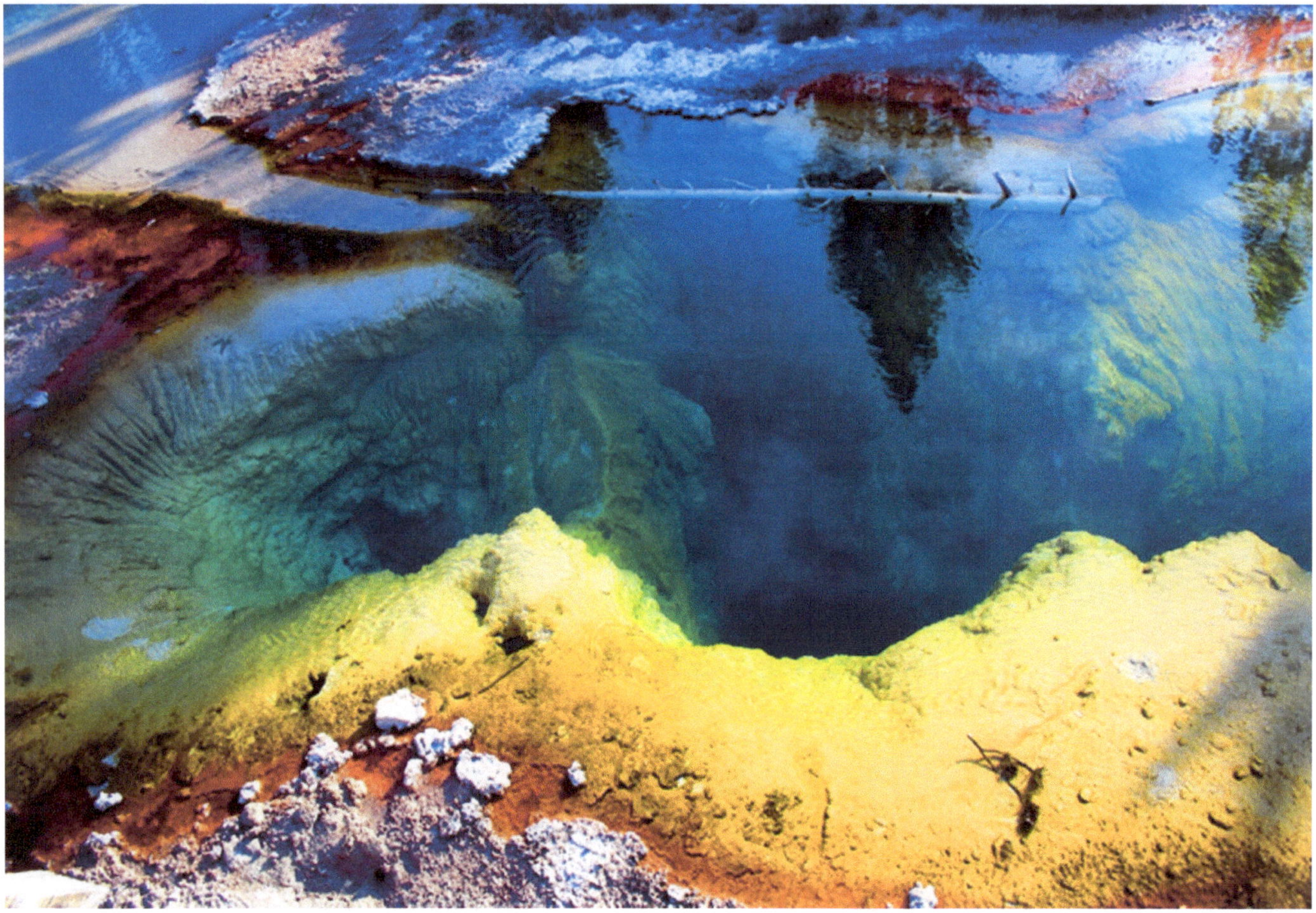

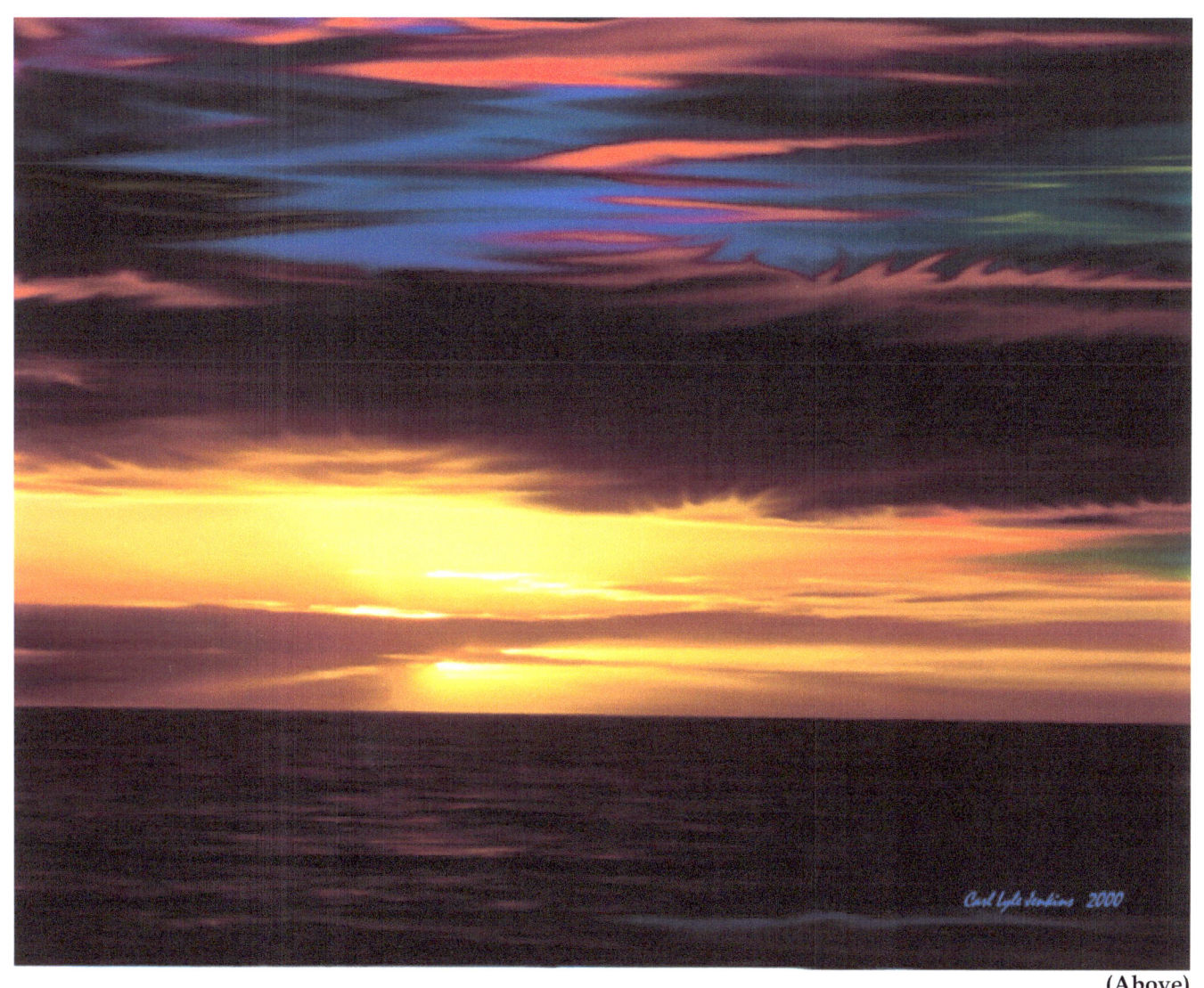

(Above)
40. *Nightfire* (Digital Image, 2000)

(Left)
39. *Thermal Pond, Yellowstone National Park* (Photo, 2010)

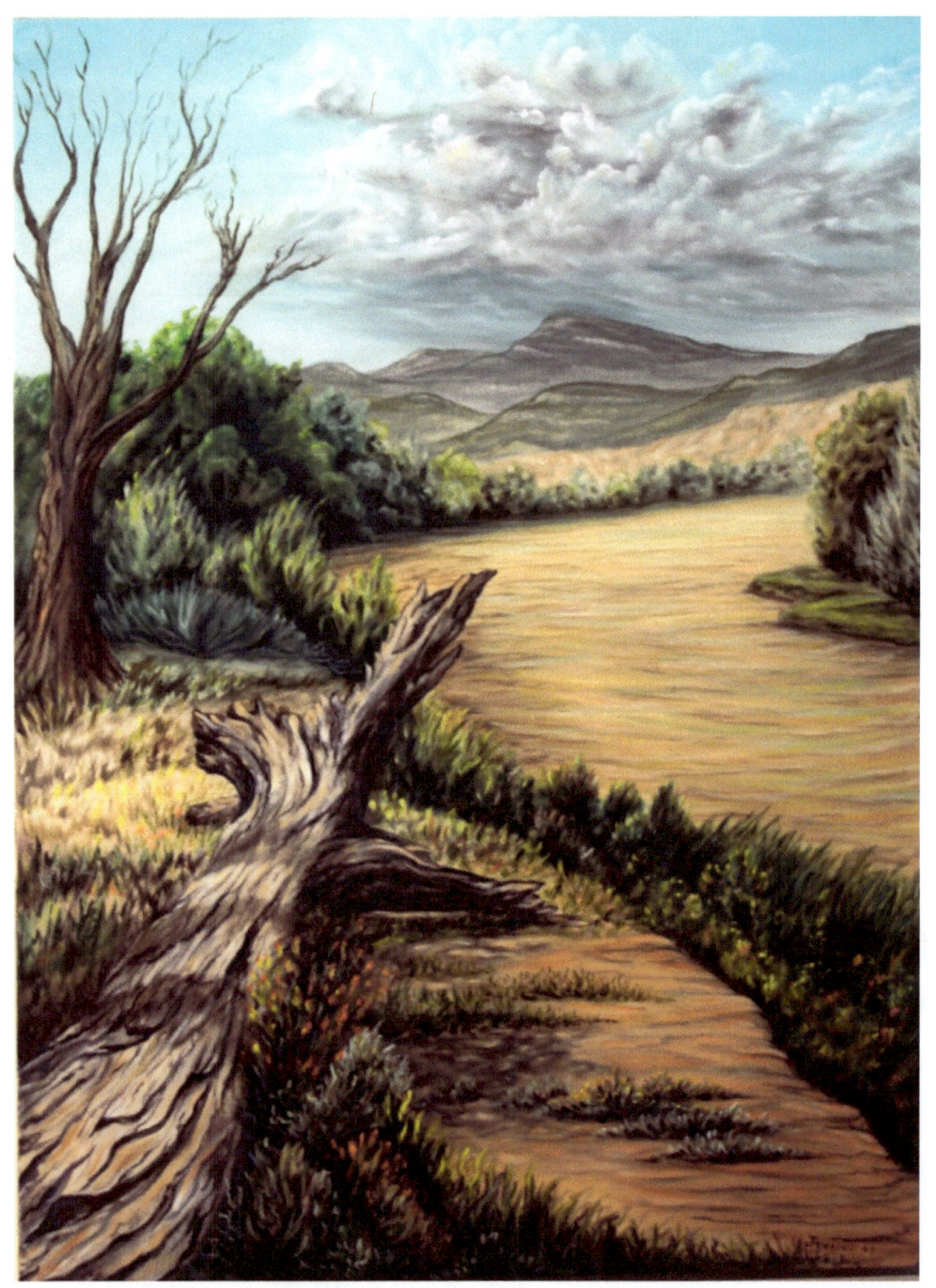

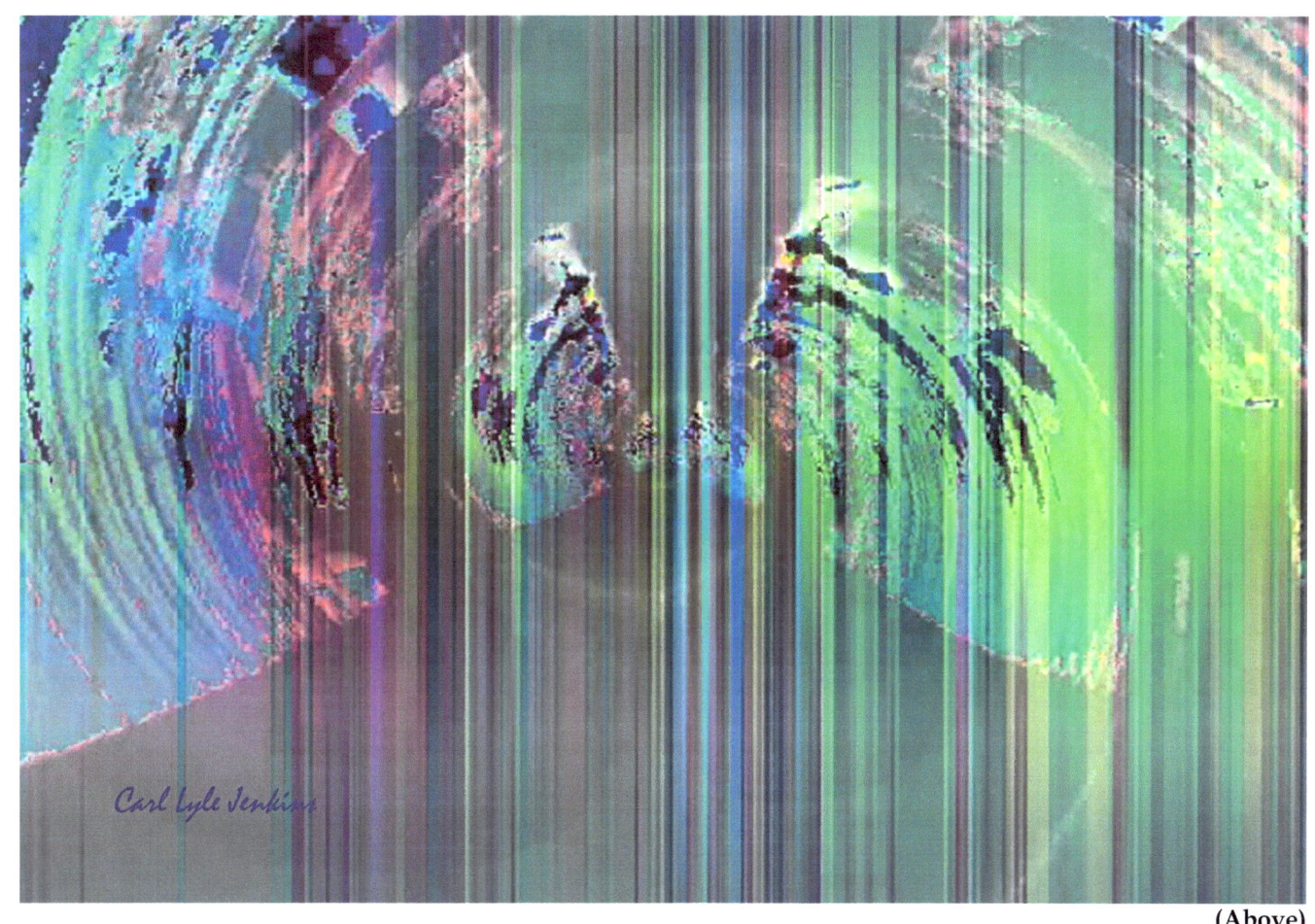

(Above)

42. Kiss (Digital Image, 2007)

(Left)

41. Los Luceros (Oil on Canvas, 30″ x 40″, 2008)

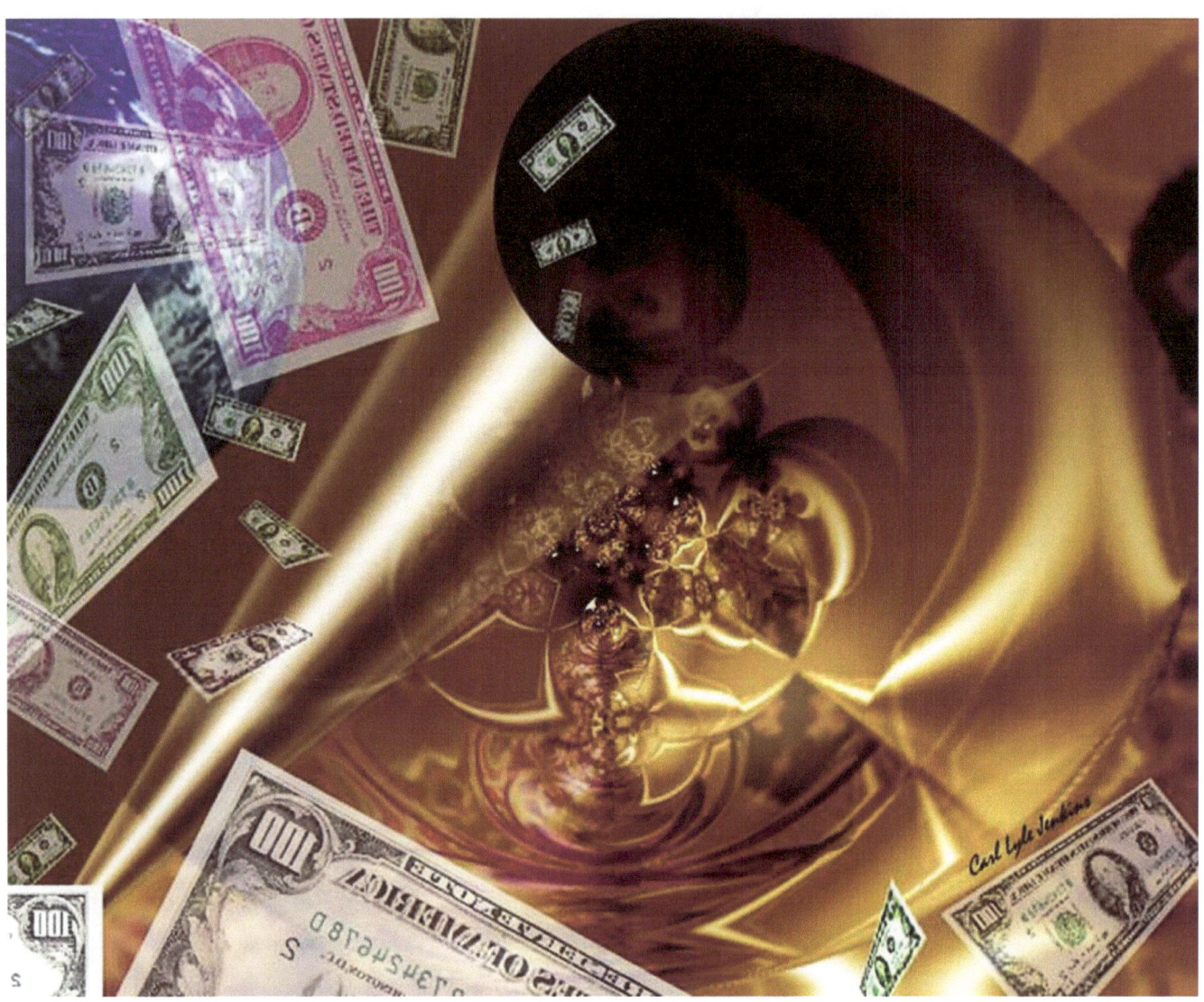

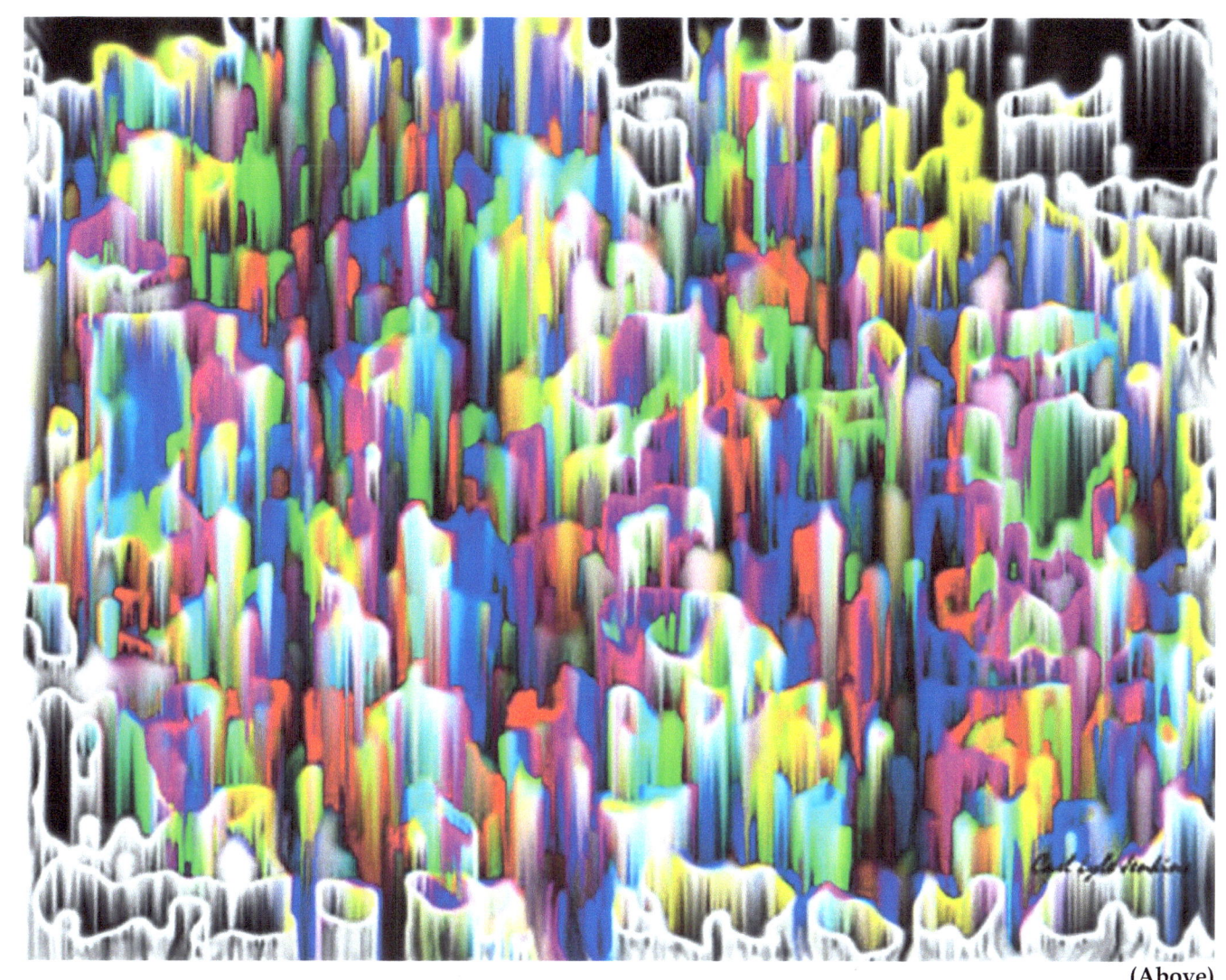

(Above)

44. *Lost in the Crowd* (Digital Image, 2002)

(Left)

43. *Funny Money* (Digital Image, 2000)

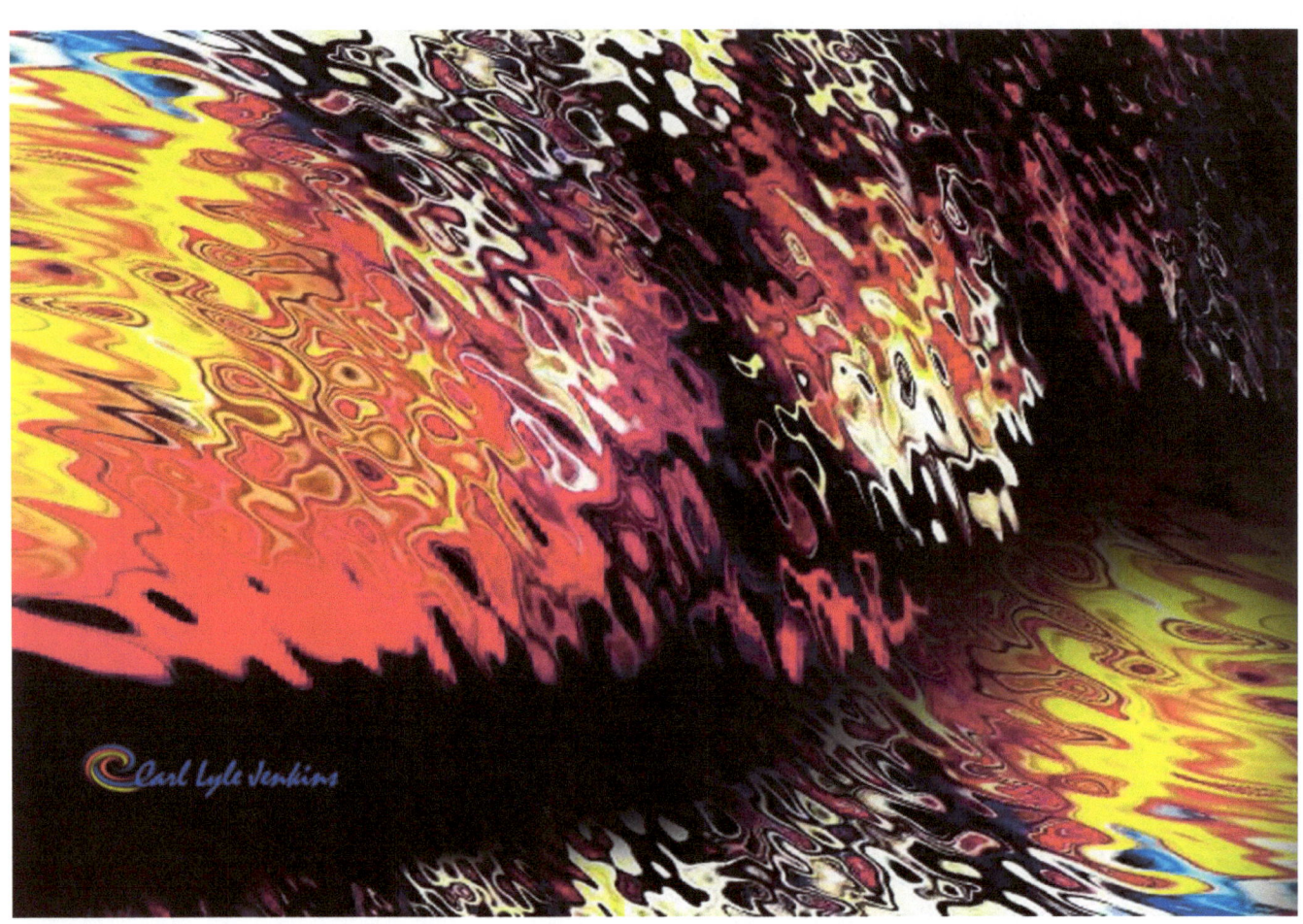

Carl Lyle Jenkins

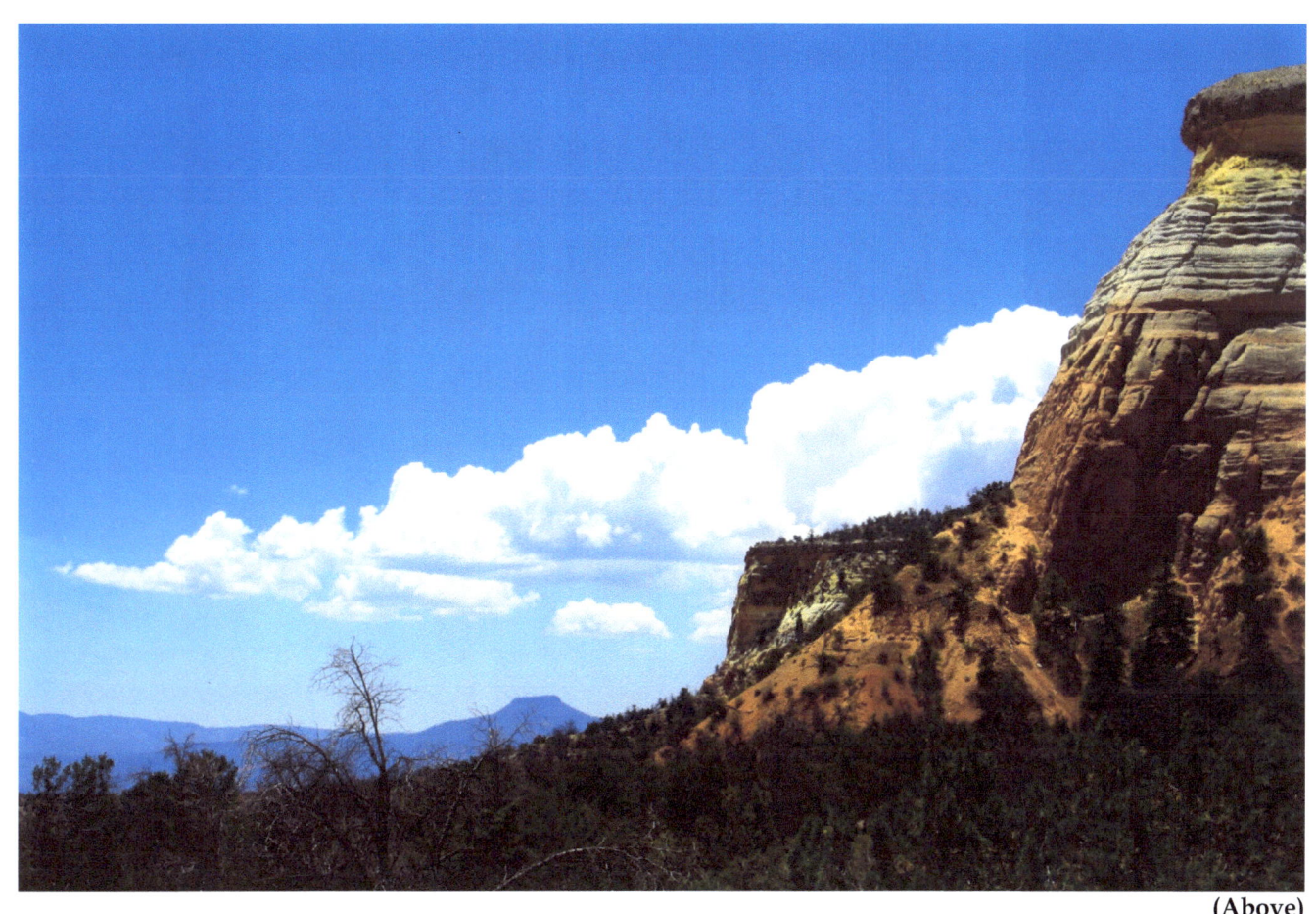

(Above)

46. Near Ghost Ranch, Northern New Mexico (Photo, 2010)

(Left)

45. New Wave (Digital Image, 2006)

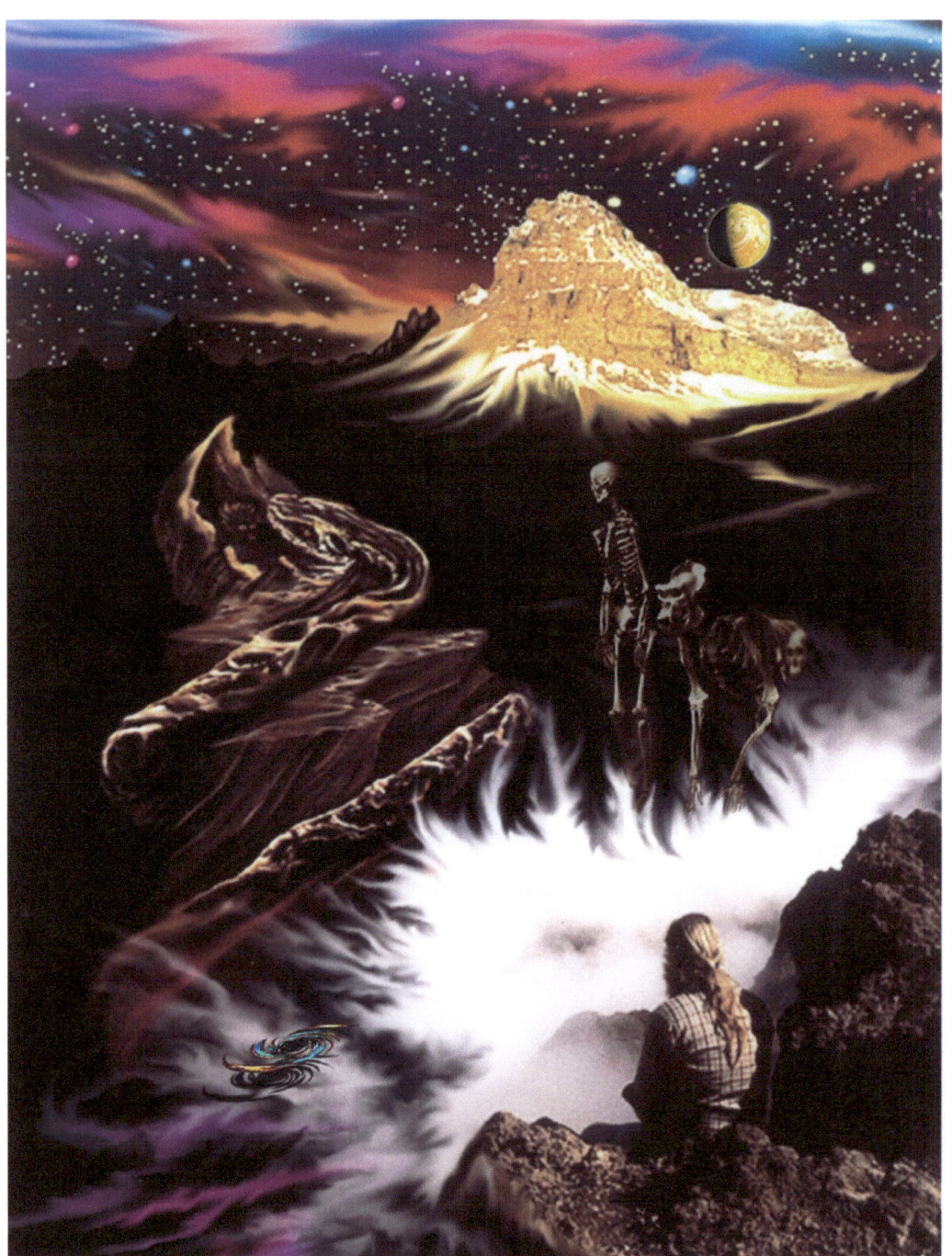

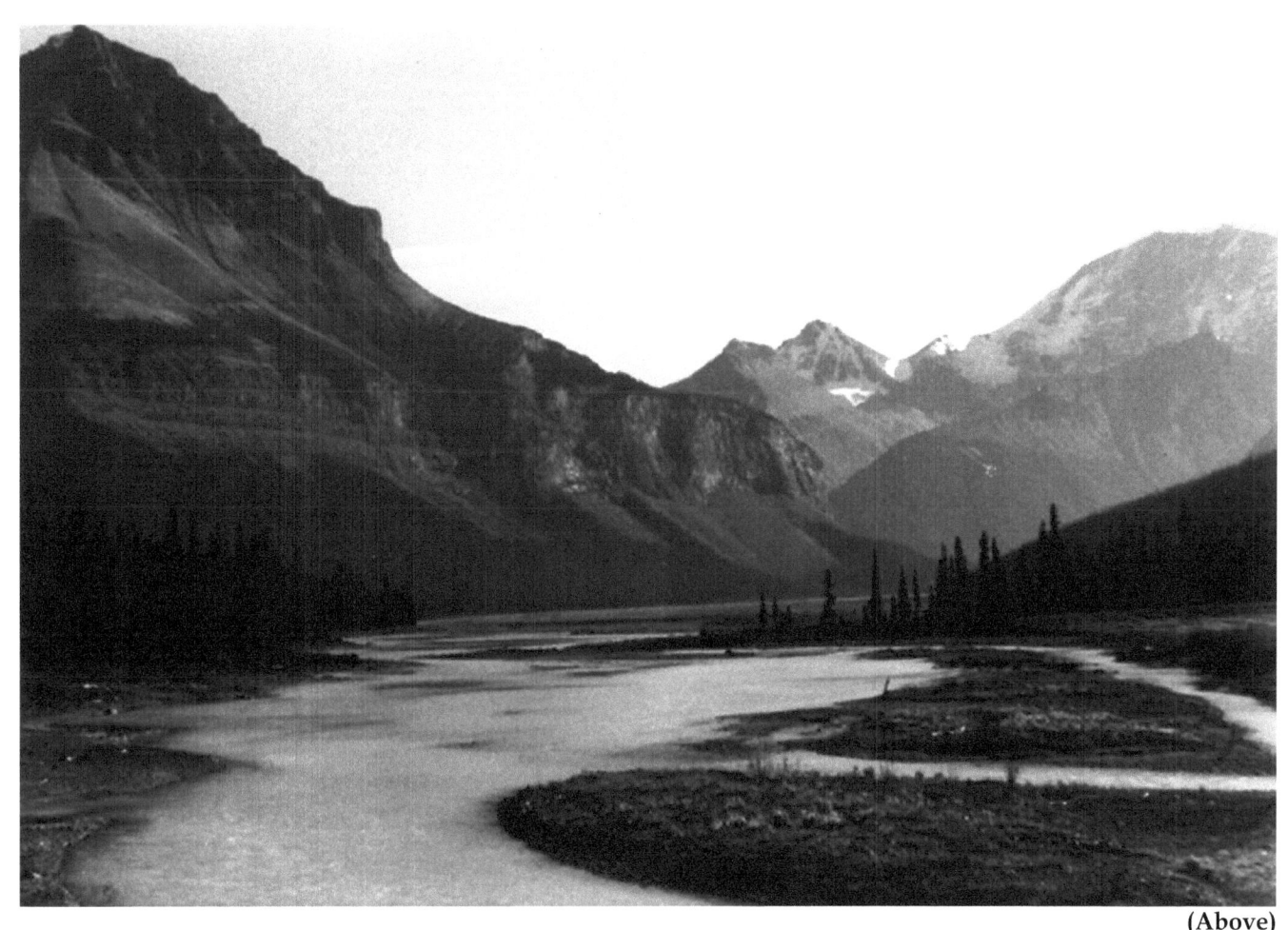

(Above)

48. *Near Jasper, Canada* (Photo, 1989)

(Left)

47. *Haleakala Dreaming—Snake of Self* (Digital Image, 1998)

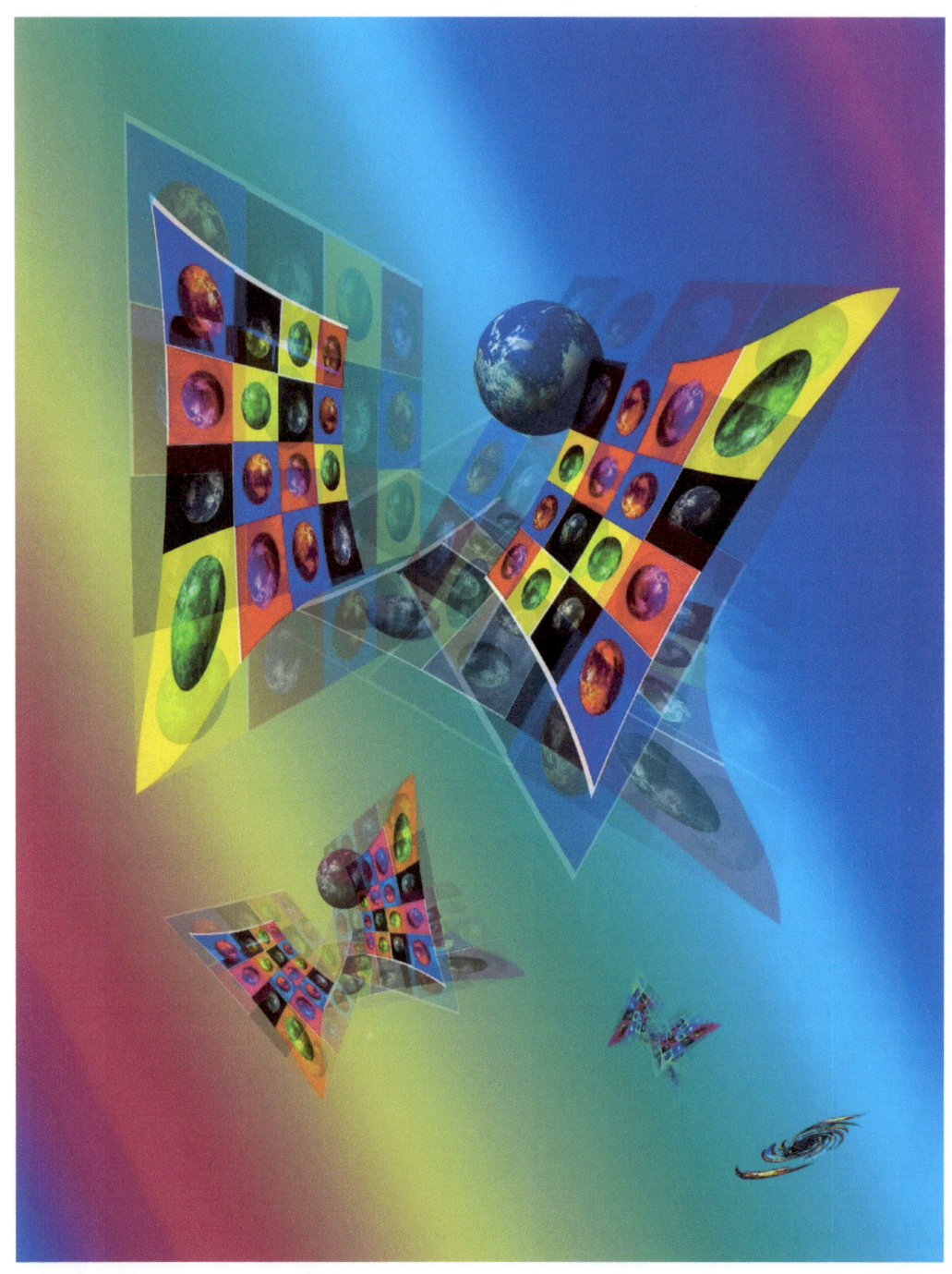

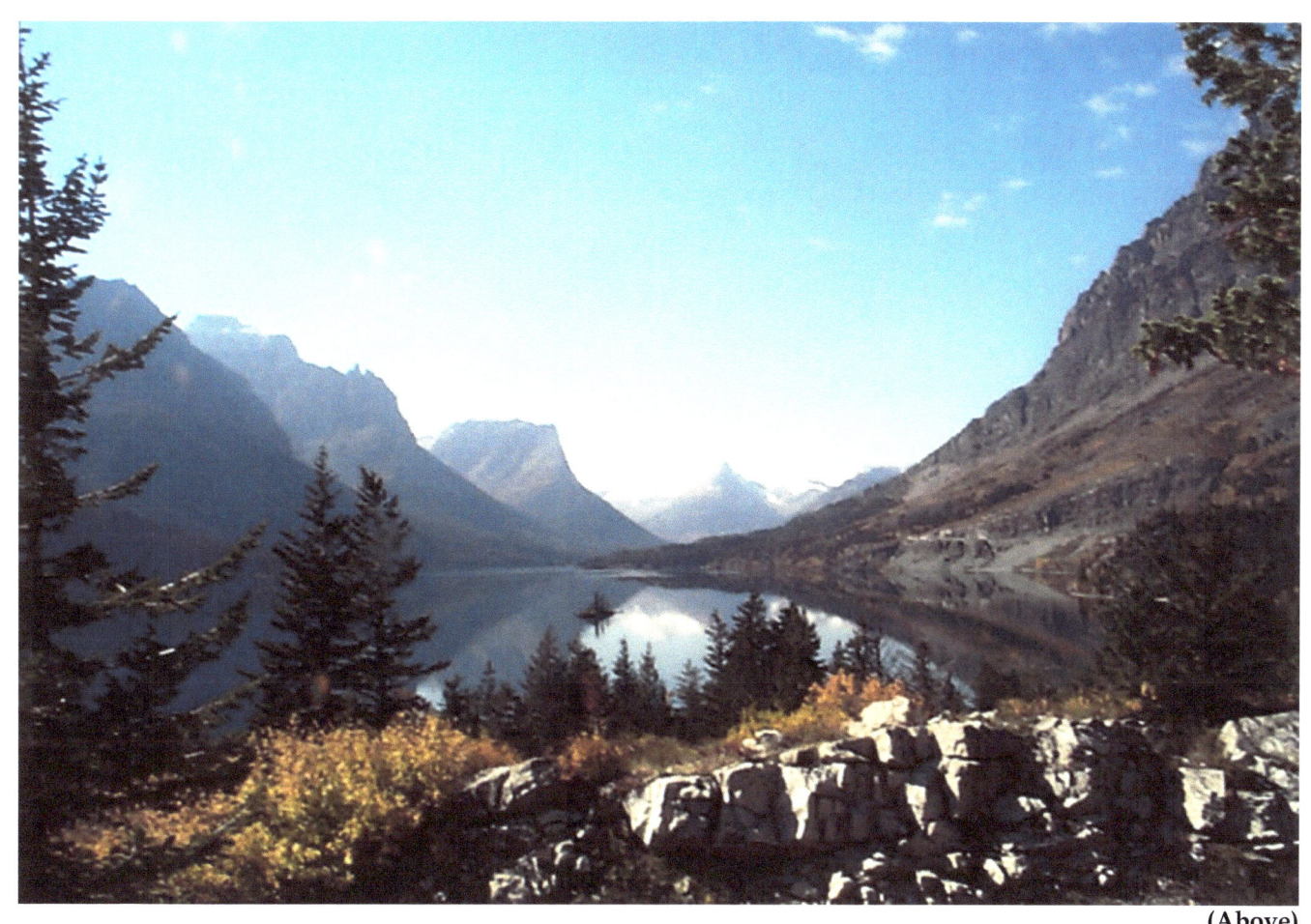

(Above)

50. Mosquito Island, Lake St. Mary, Glacier National Park, USA (Photo, 2007)

(Left)
49. New Dimensions (Digital Image, 2004)

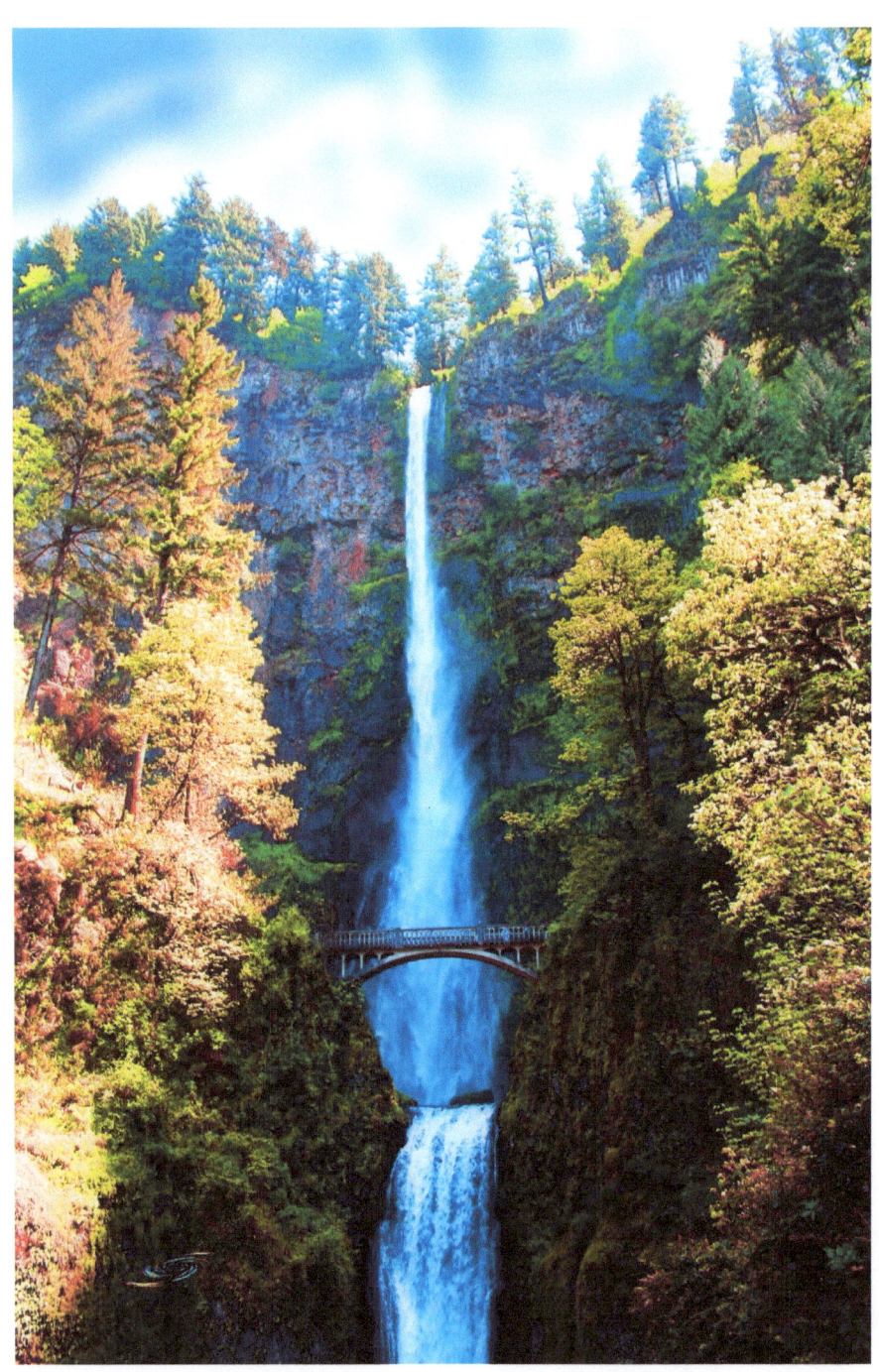

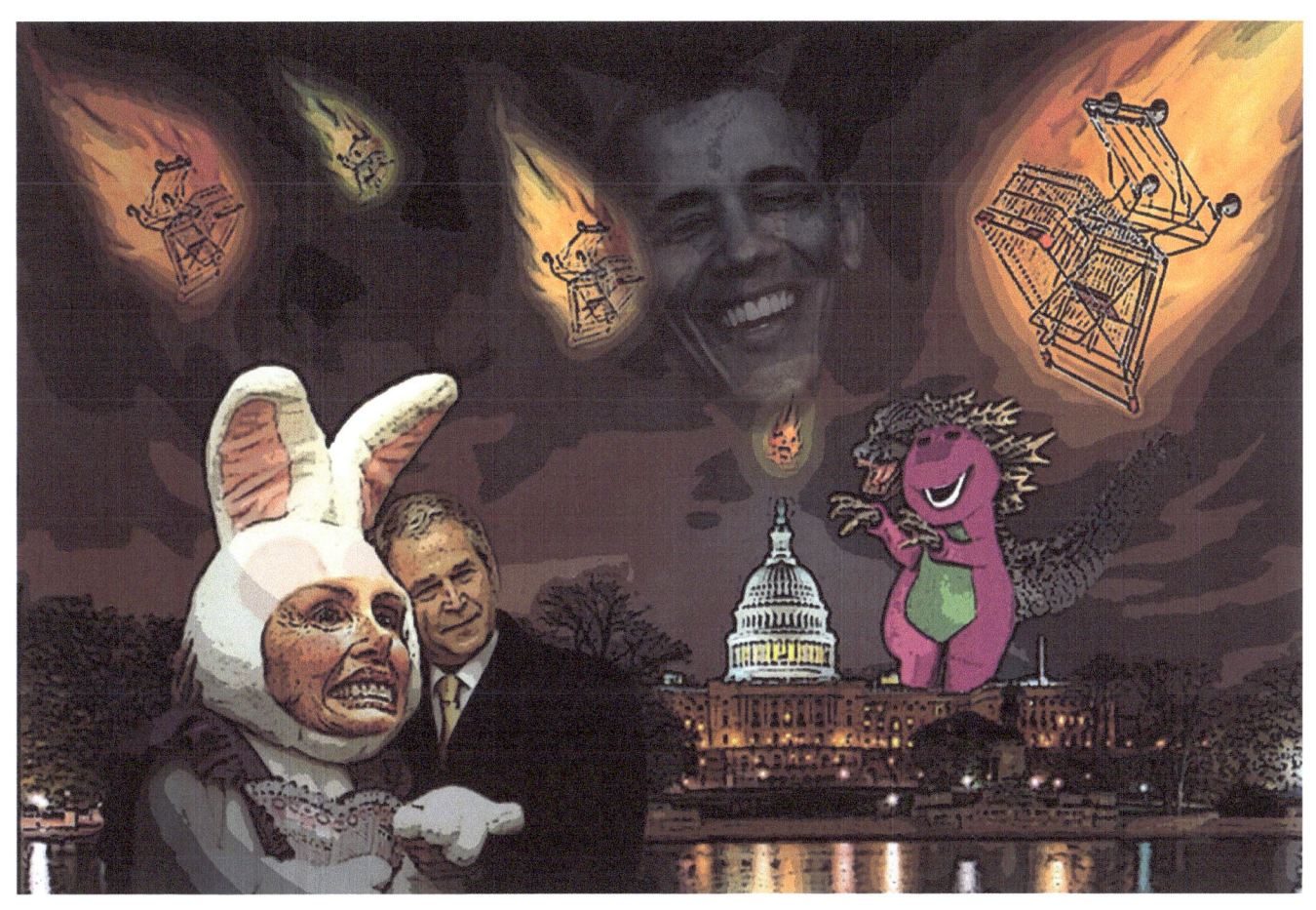

(Above)

52. Nightmare on the Plaza (Digital Image, 2008)

(Left)

51. Cascade (Digital Image, 2005)

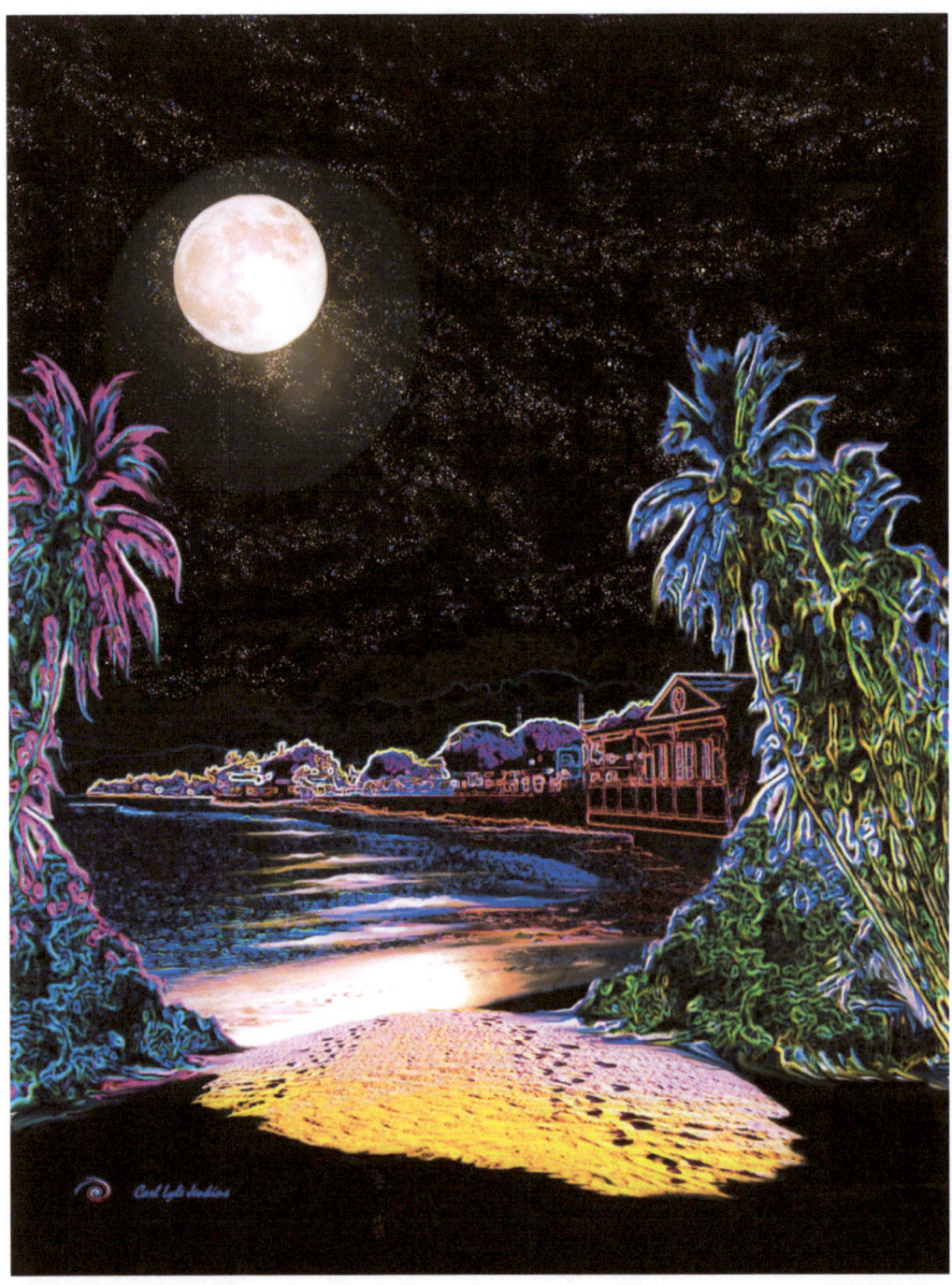

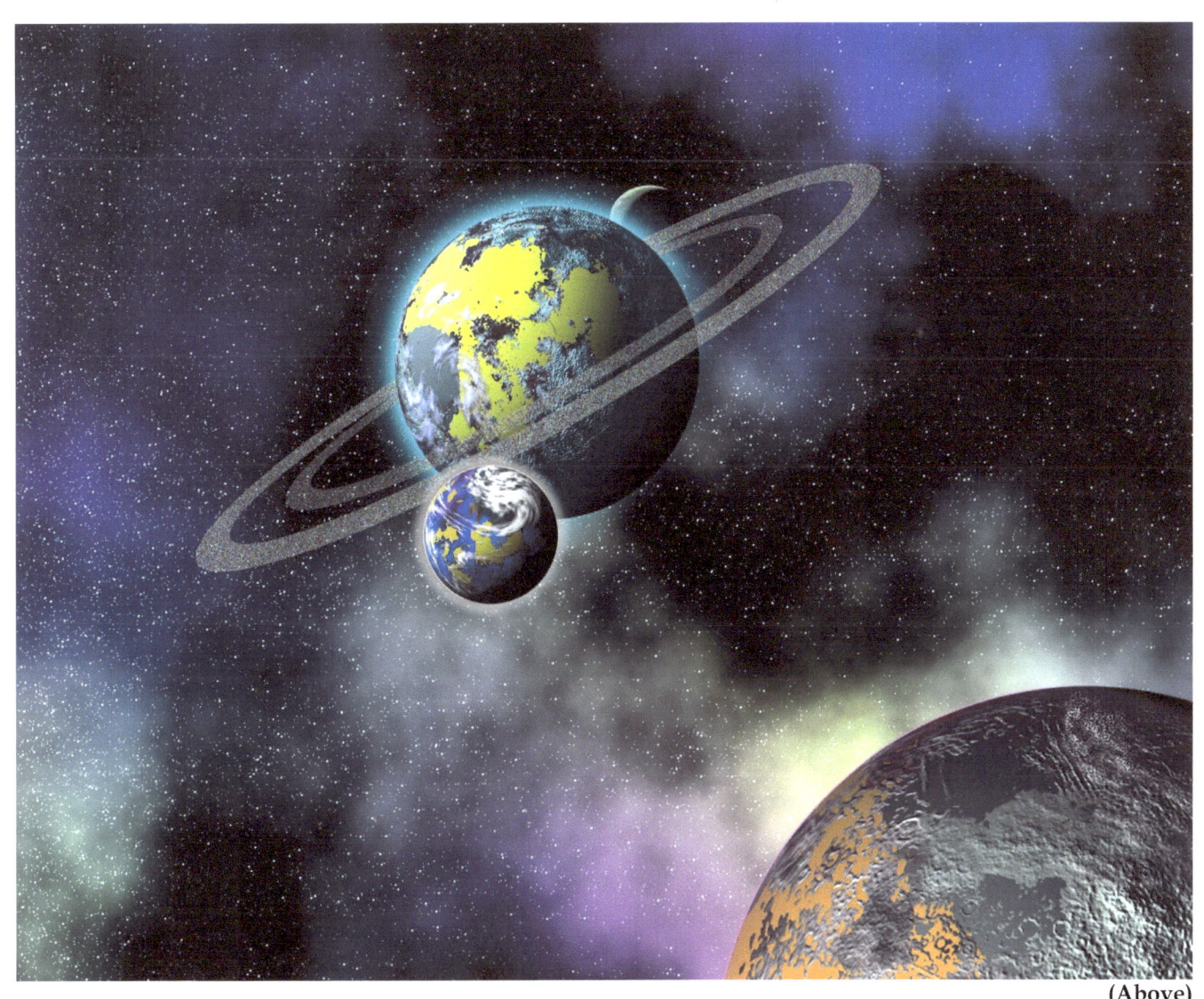

(Above)

54. *Planet Dance* (Digital Image, 2004)

(Left)

53. *Lahaina Luna* (Digital Image, 2002)

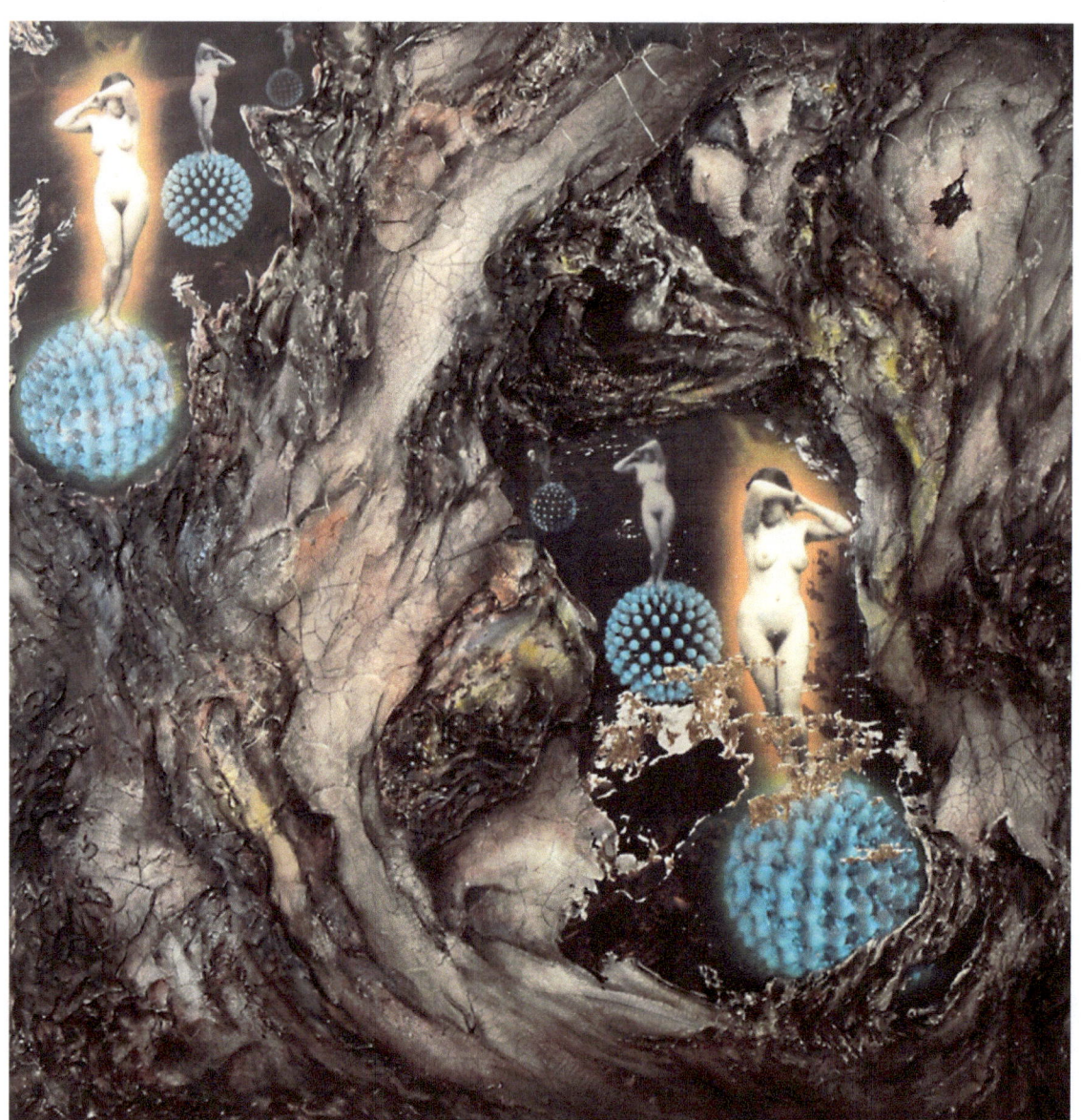

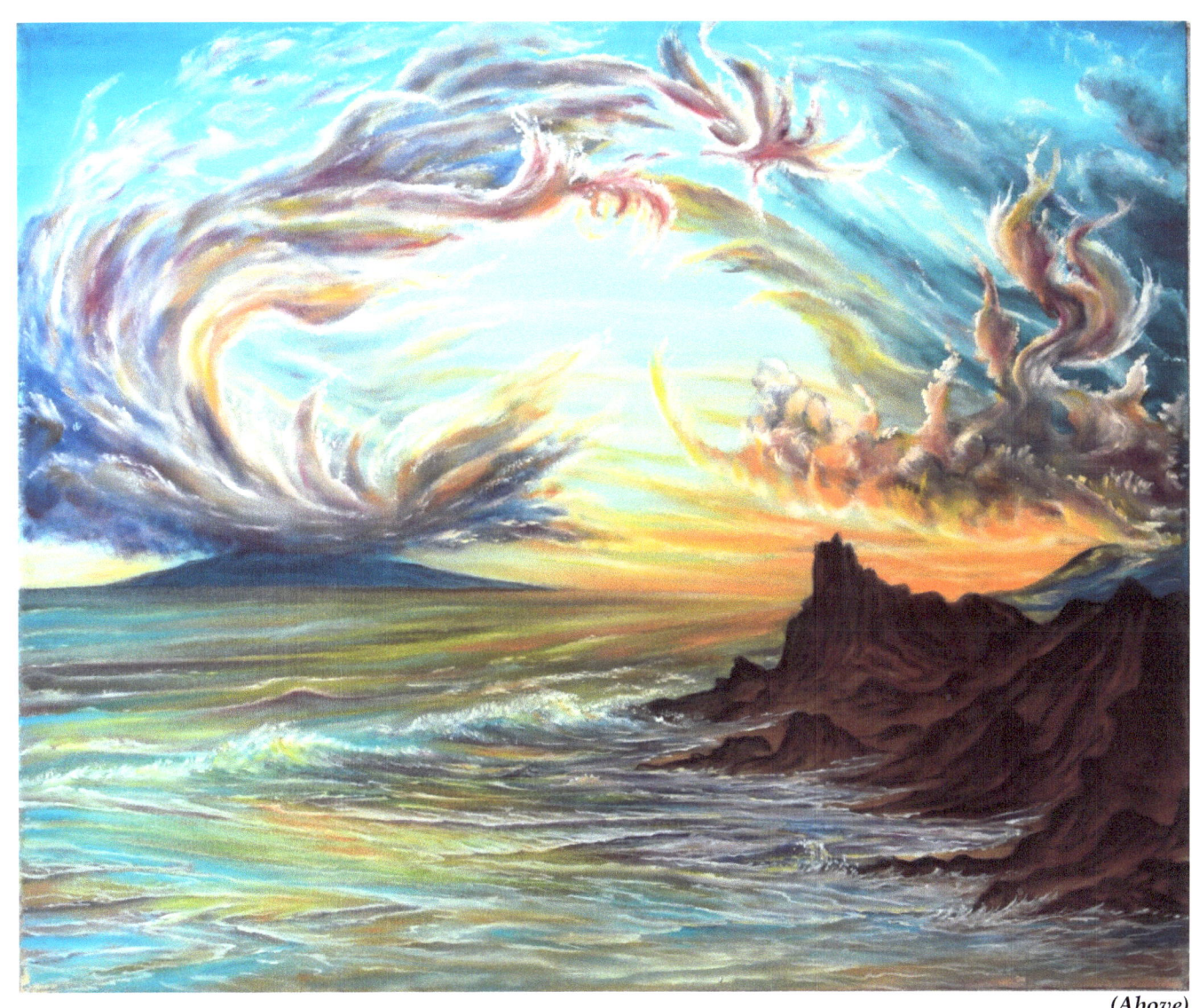

(Above)

56. *Flowers From Pele* (Oil on Canvas, 24″ x 30″, 1998)

(Left)

55. *Seven* (Acrylic/Mixed Media on Masonite, 24″ x 24″, 2015)

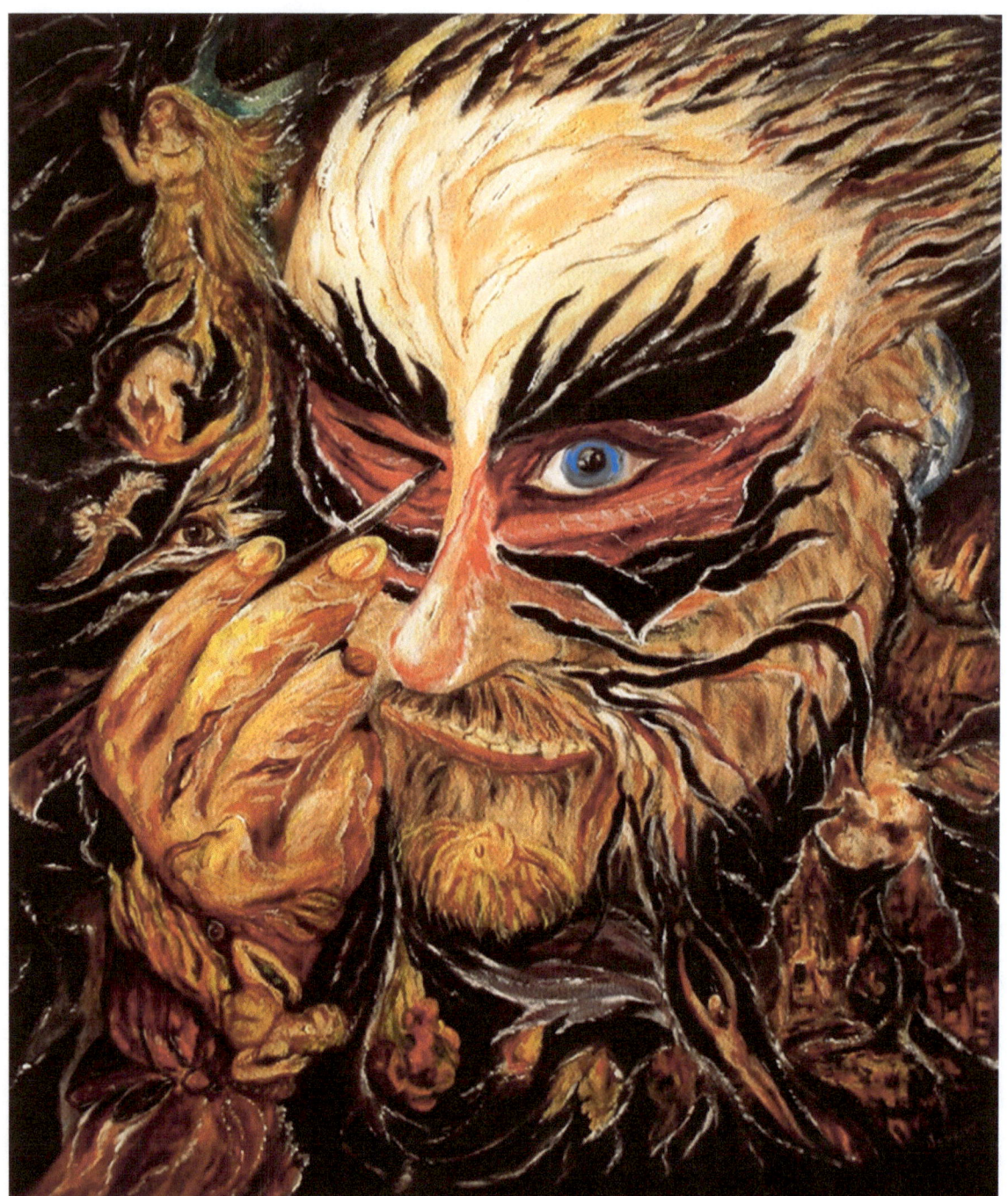

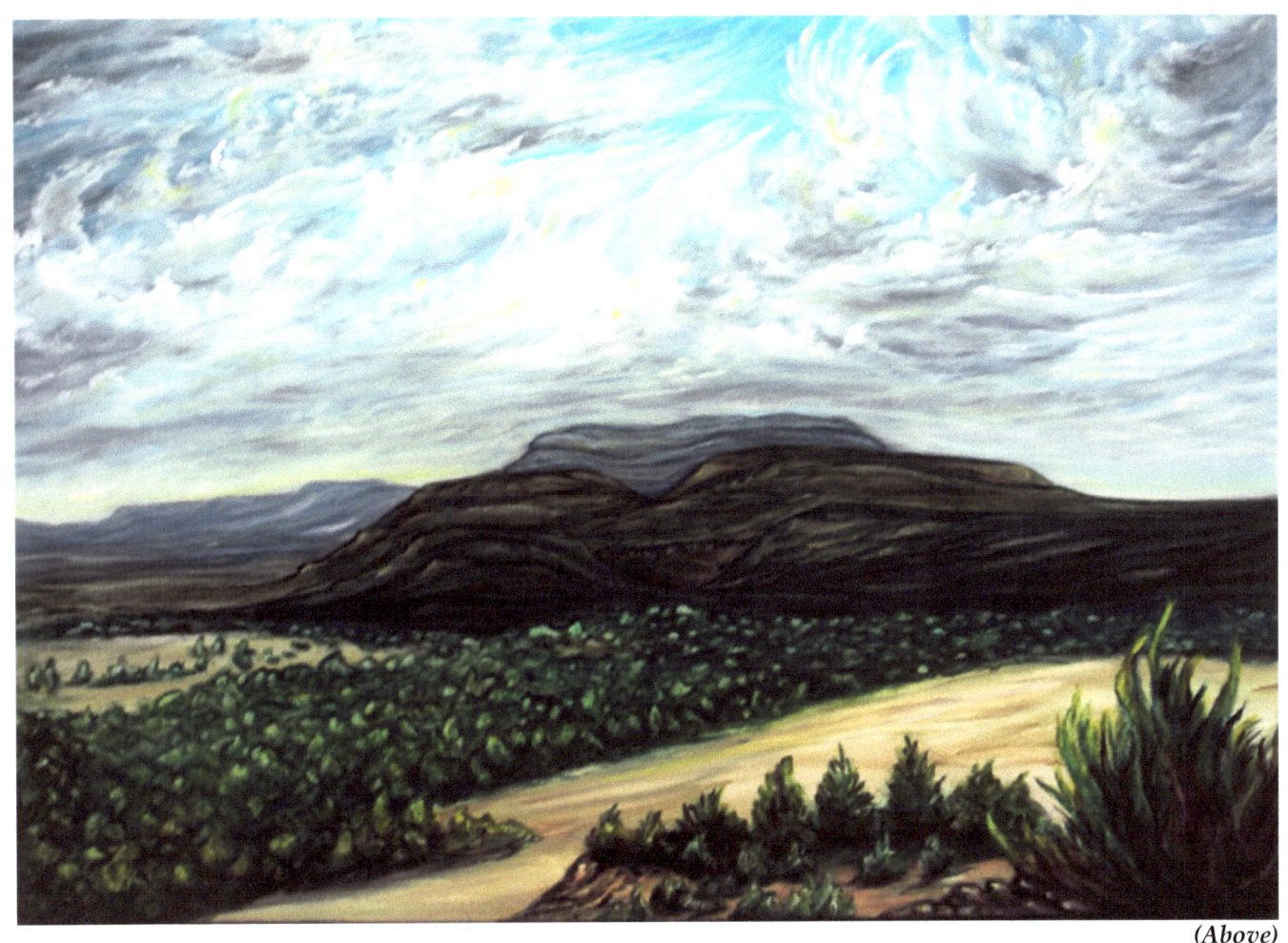

(Above)

58. *Pecos Wilderness* (Oil on Canvas, 18″ x 24″, 2008)

(Left)

57. *I Shadow* (Oil on Canvas, 18″ x 24″, 2008)

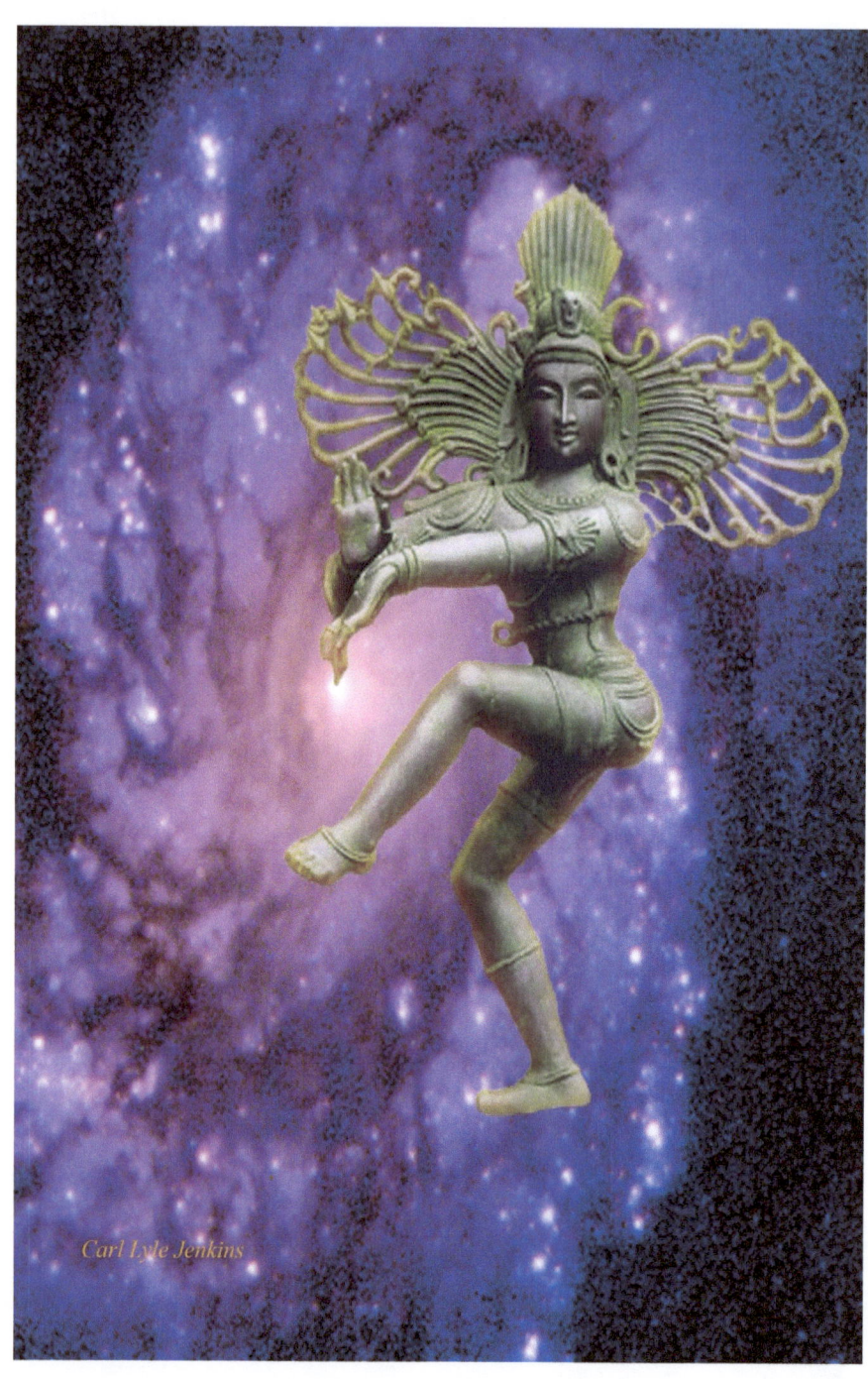

Carl Lyle Jenkins

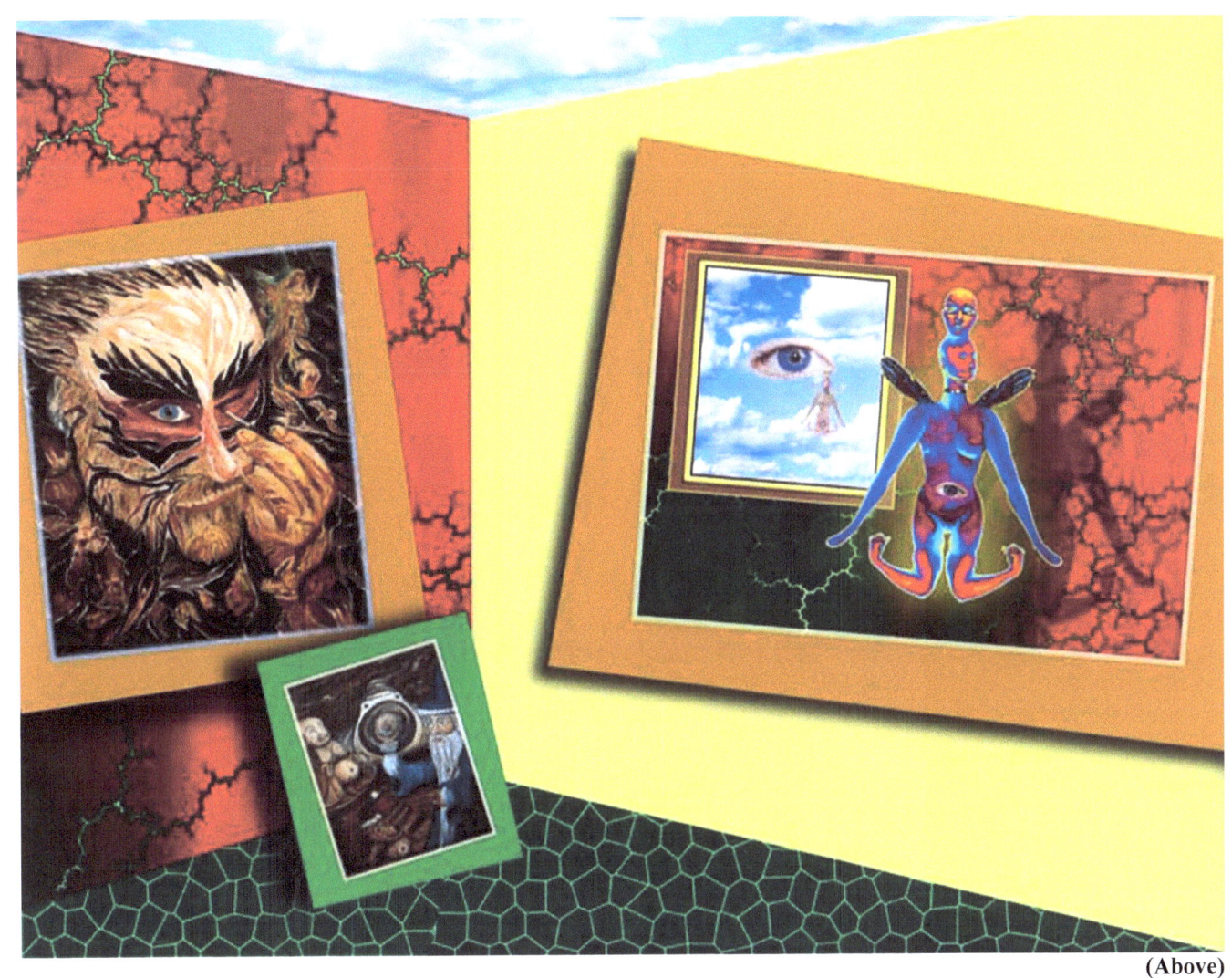

(Above)

60. *Gallery* (Acrylic/Mixed Media on Canvas, 30″ x 40″, 2014)

(Left)

59. *Shiva* (Digital Image, 2010)

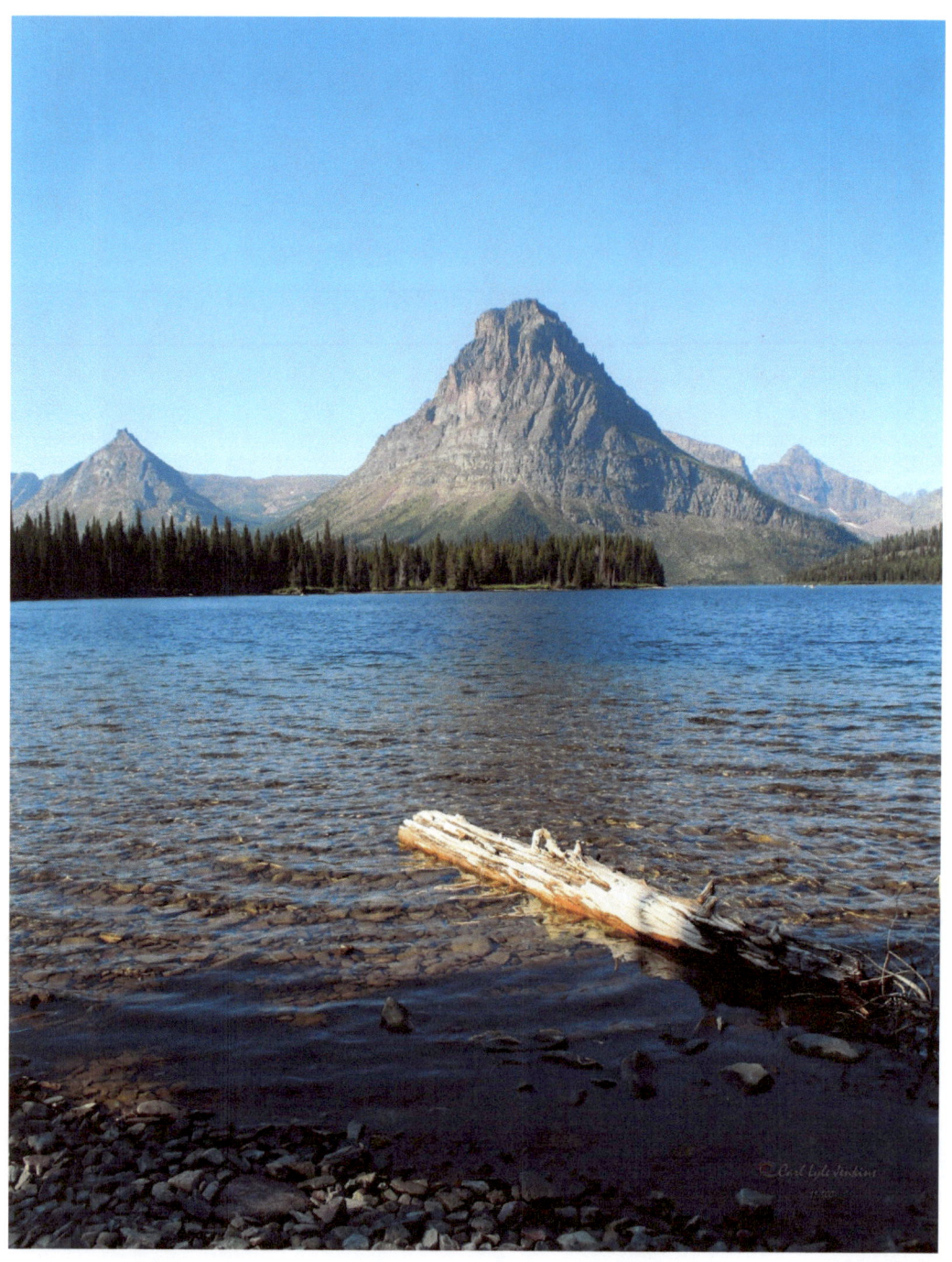

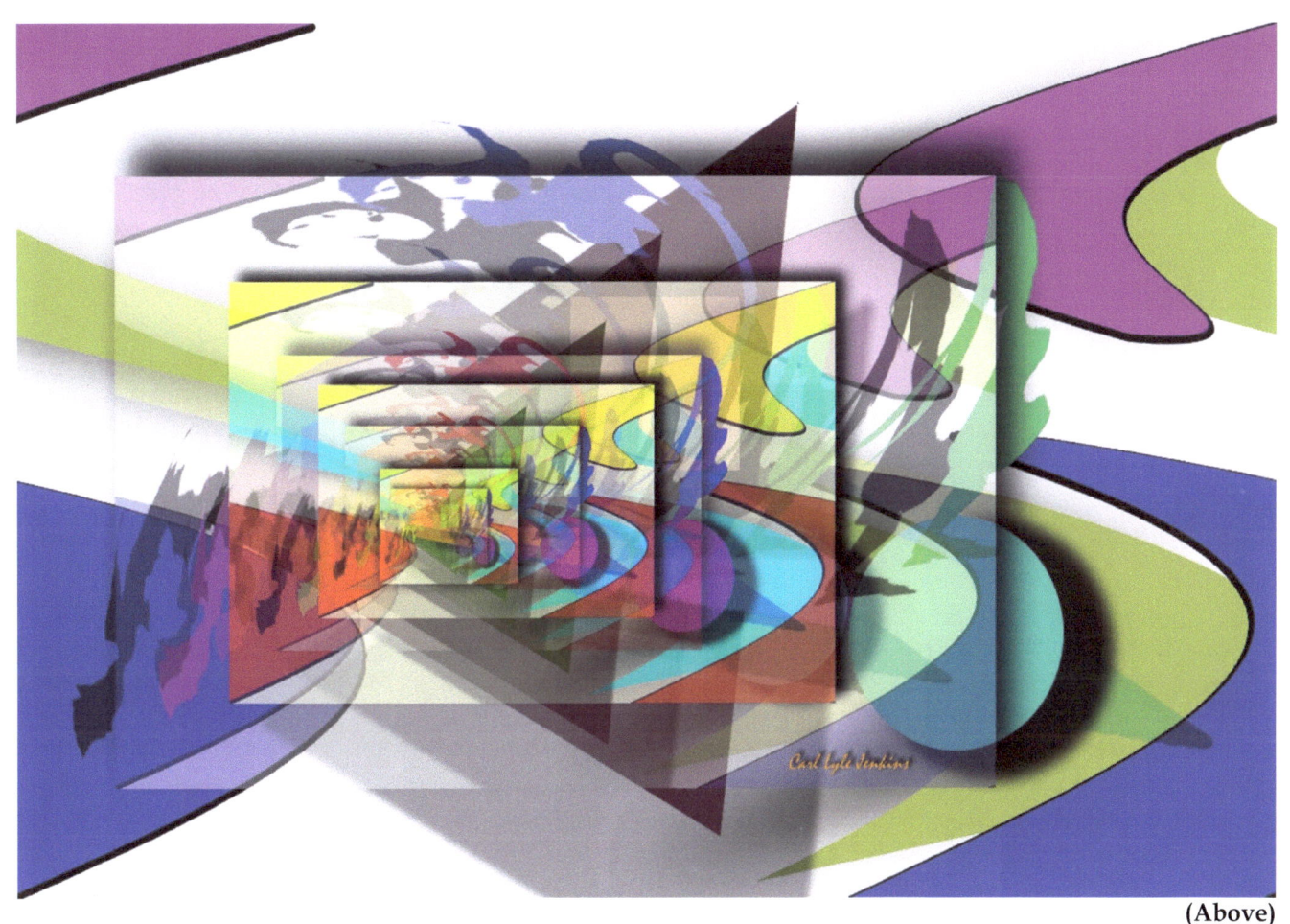

(Above)
62. Corridor (Digital Image 2014)

(Left)
61. Summer, Two Medicine Lake, Glacier National Park, USA (Photo, 2010)

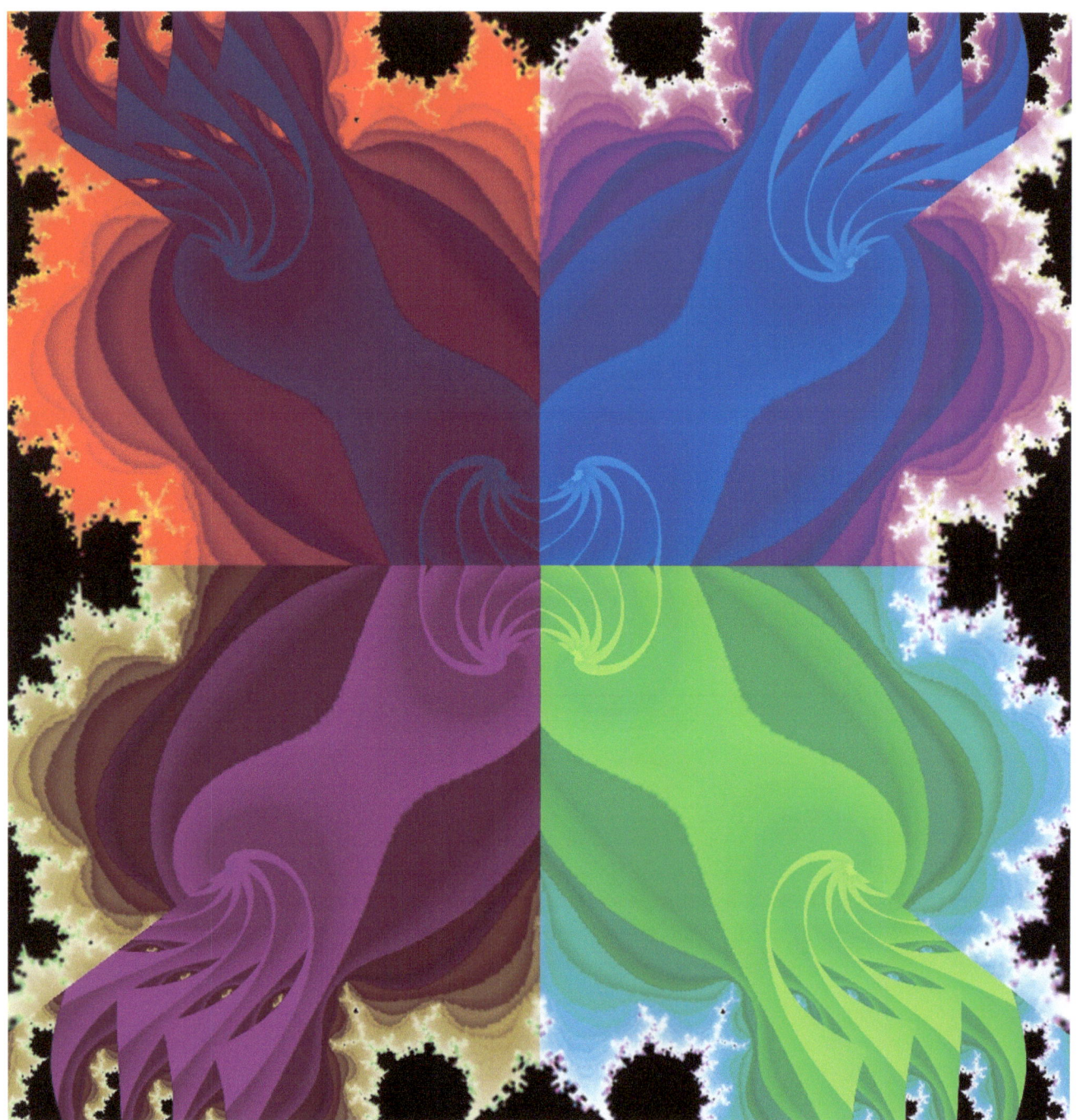

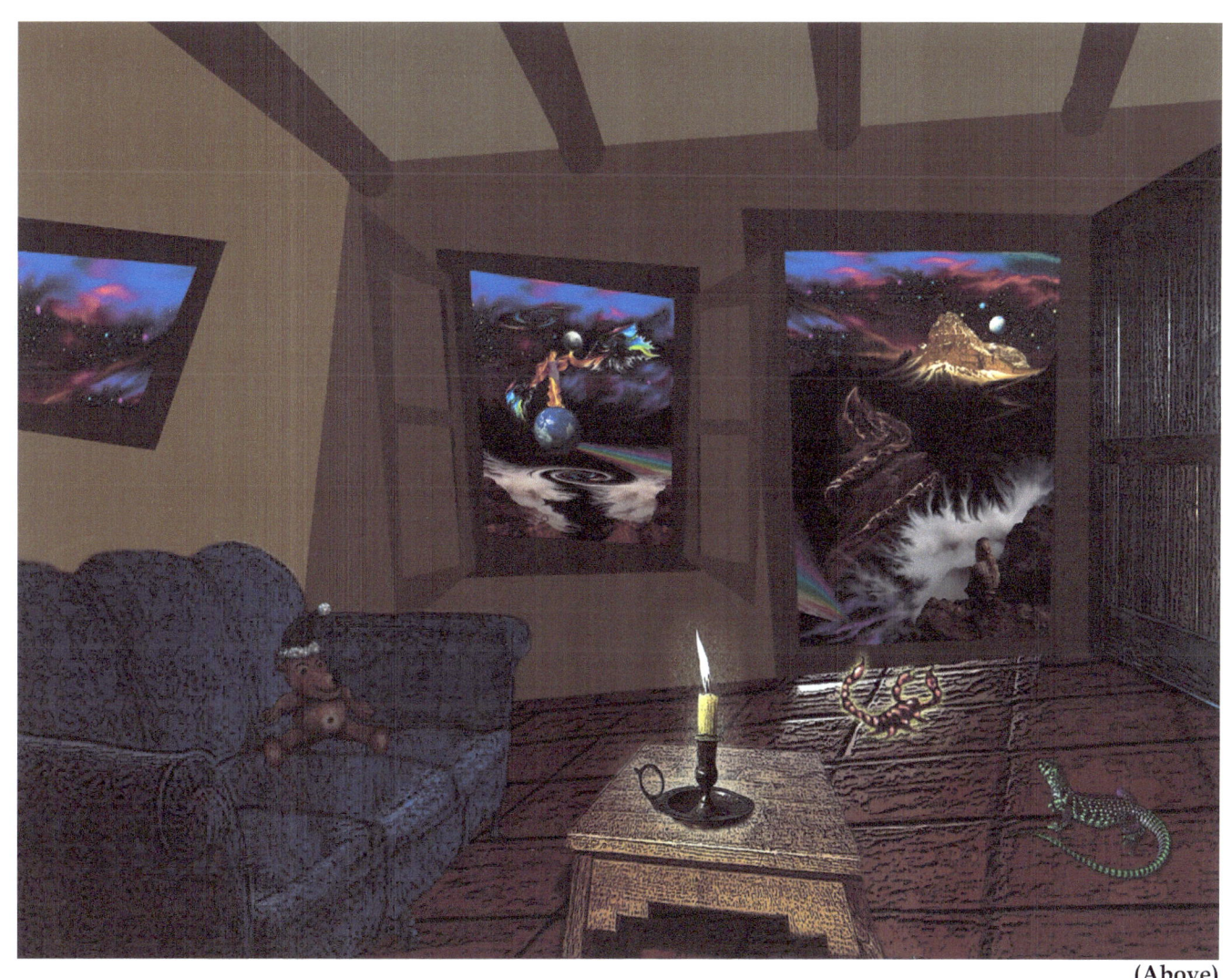

(Above)

64. Spooky Night (Digital Image, 2014)

(Left)

63. Square Dancer (Digital Image, 2014)

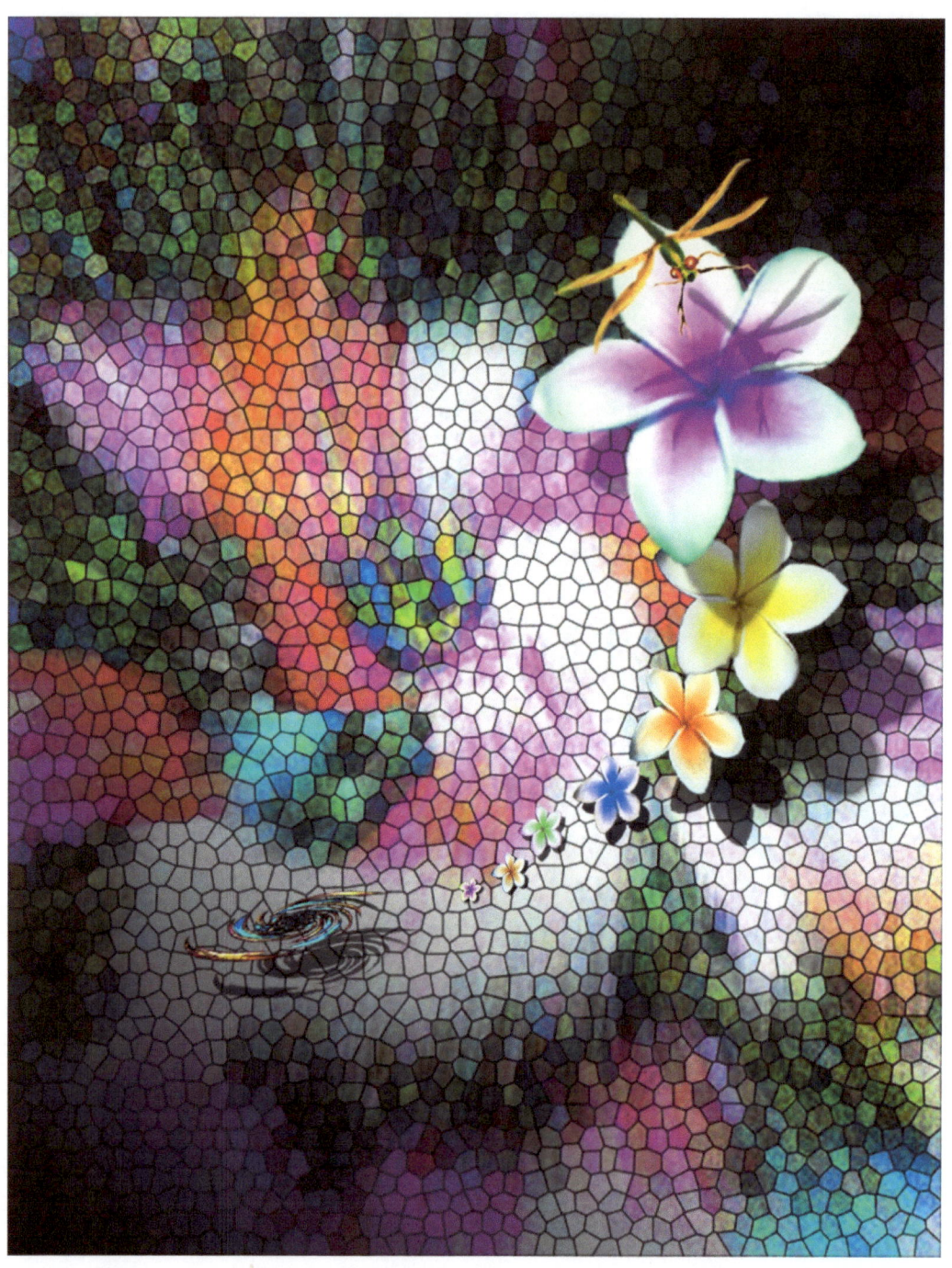

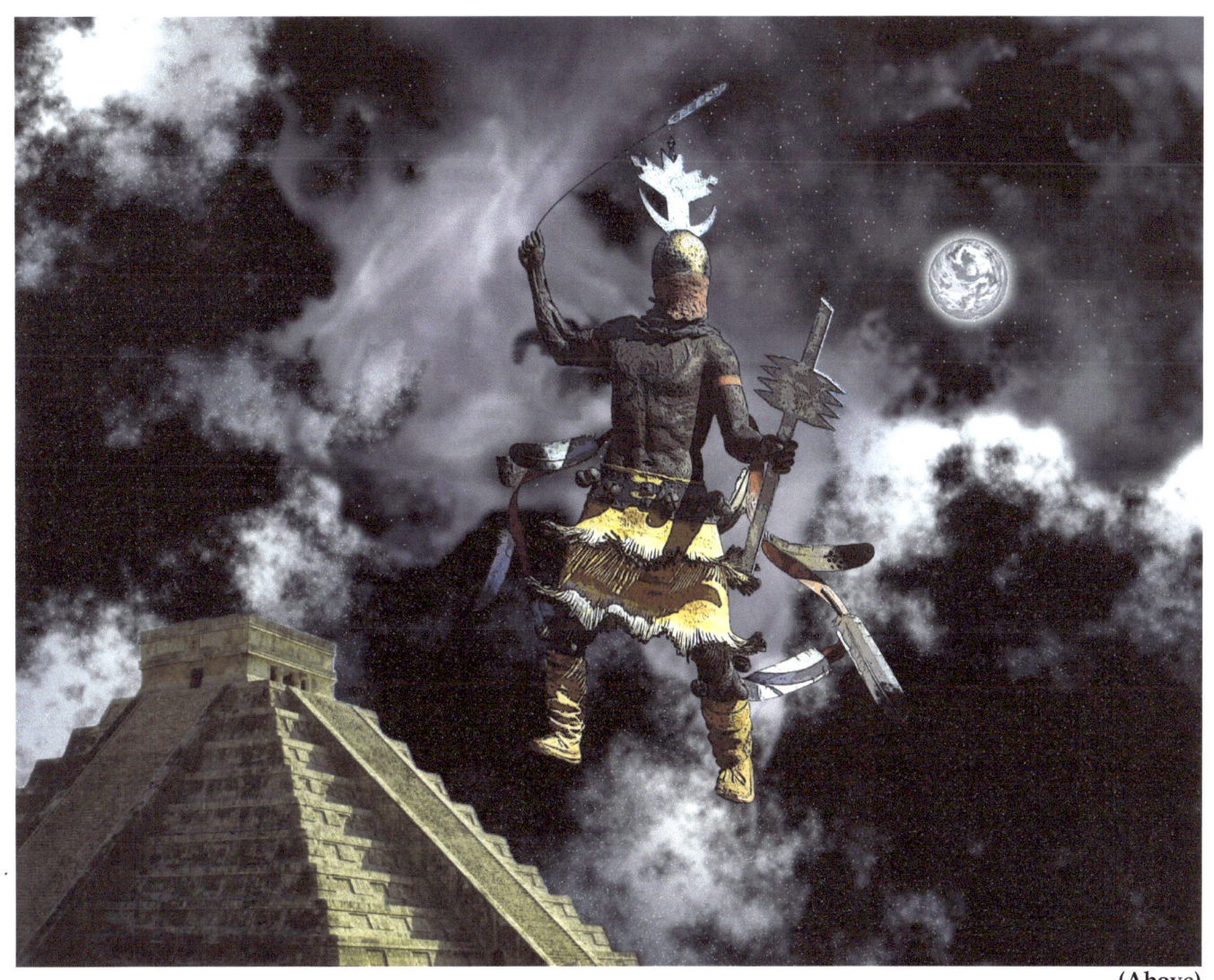

(Above)

66. *Fabled and Forbidden Lands* (Digital Image, 2015)

(Left)

65. *Dragonfly's Dream* (Digital Image, 2006)

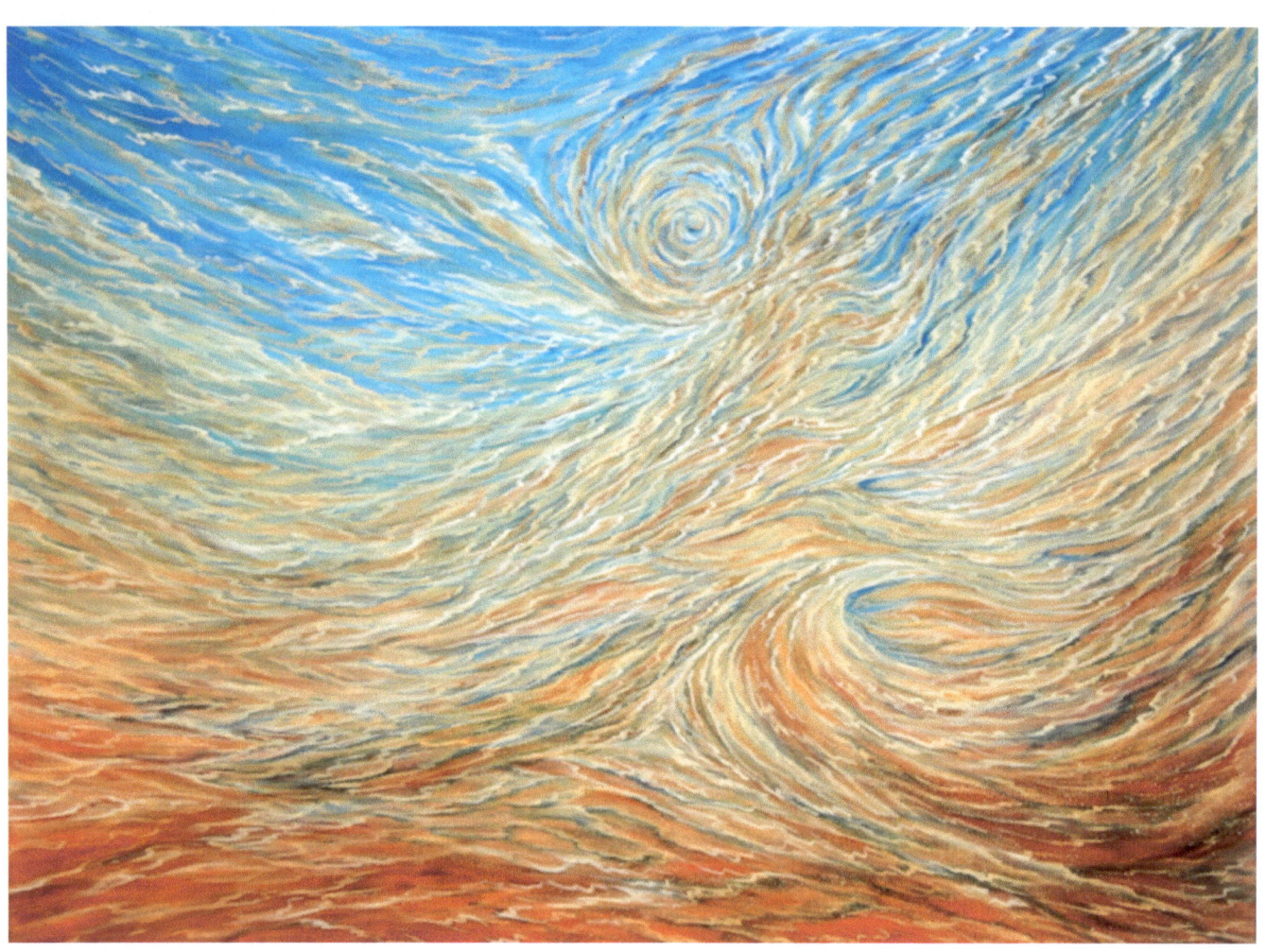

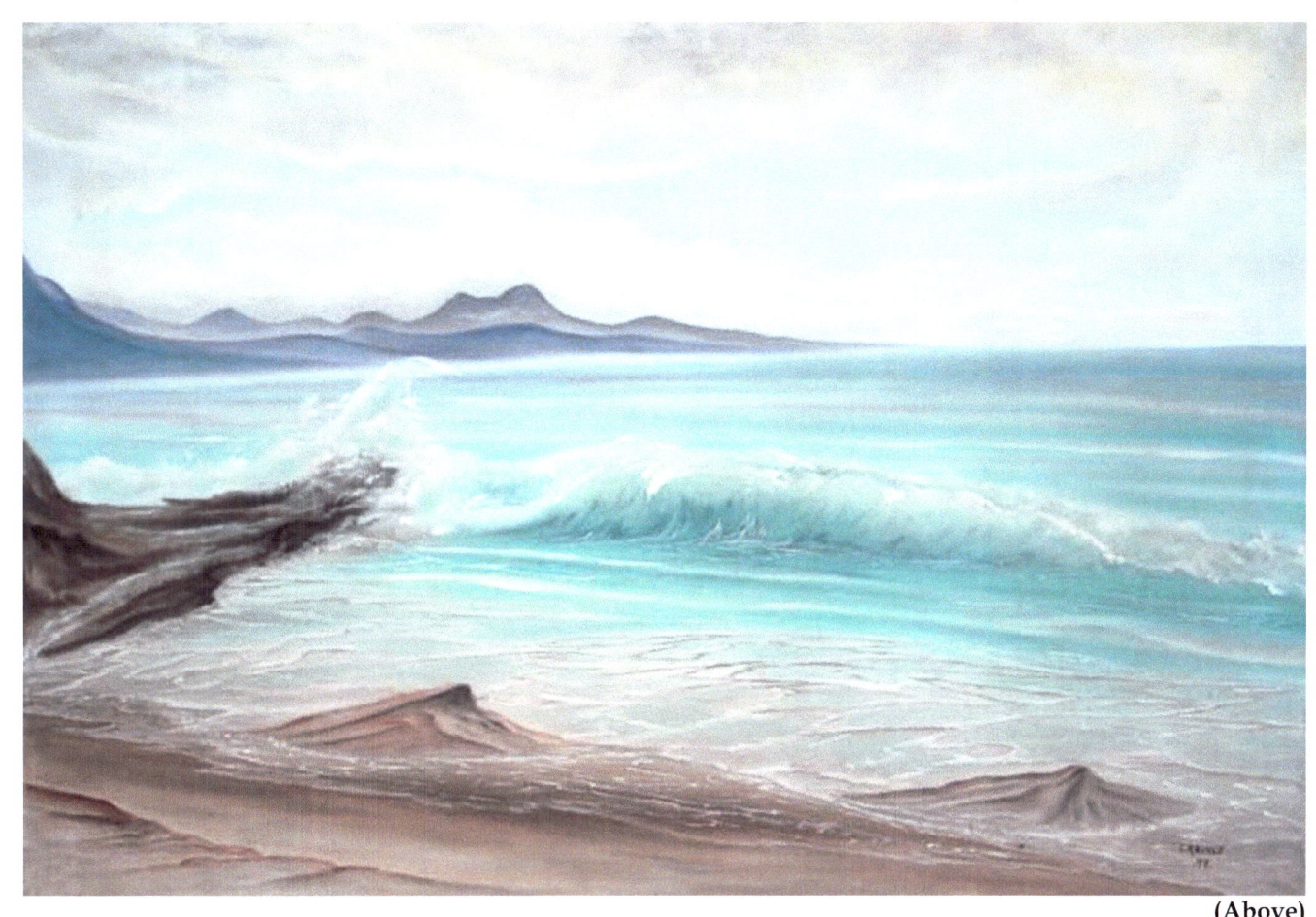

(Above)

68. *Santa Cruz* (Oil on Canvas, 24″ x 36″, 1977)

(Left)

67. *Desert Sands* (Oil on Canvas, 30″ x 40″, 2010)

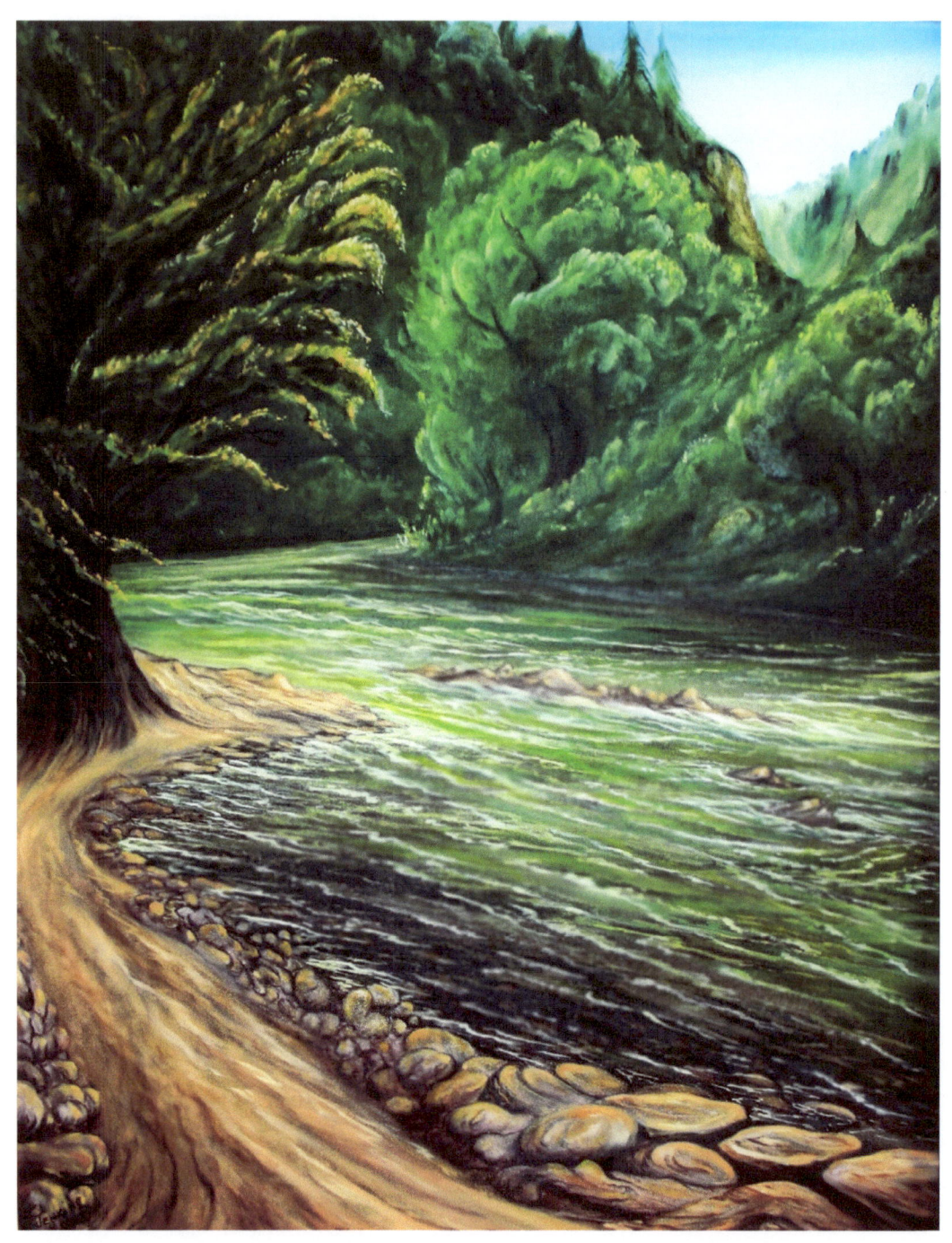

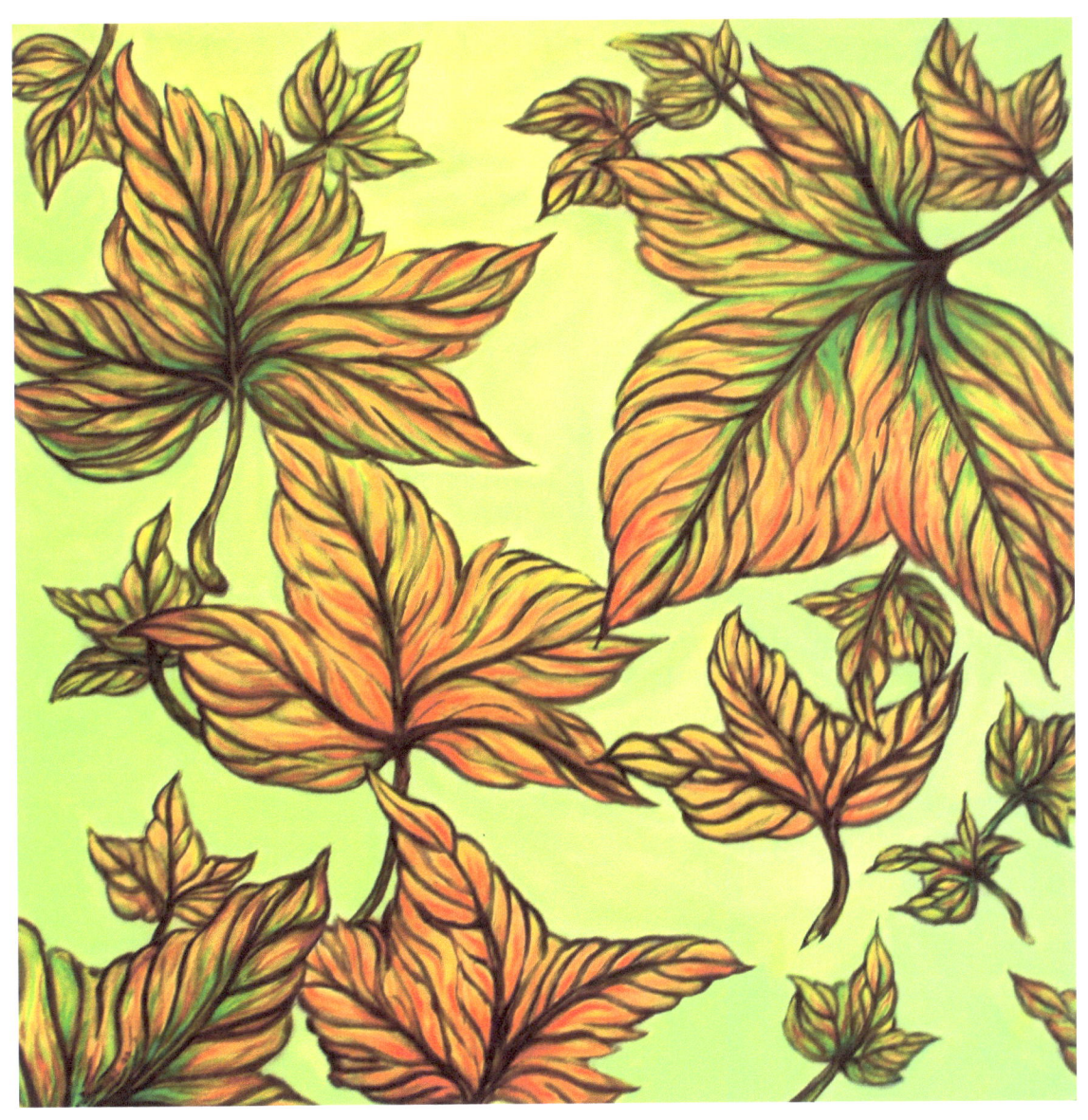

70. *Fall* (Oil on Canvas, 30″ x 30″, 2007)

69. *Pecos River* (Oil on Canvas, 24″ x 30″, 2008)

About Carl Lyle Jenkins

Carl Lyle Jenkins has been an artist for his entire life. He won his first award for his artistic creations at the age of eight in a countywide fire-safety poster contest. Carl sold his first oil painting, a seascape, at age twelve! Since then he has created hundreds of original works of art including a number of murals in public and private places. Carl exhibited and sold his art for years through the noted Lahaina Arts Society Galleries and their weekly Banyan Tree Art Shows in Lahaina, Hawaii. His artwork has been purchased by collectors from around the world.

The images presented in *Imagician* include oil paintings, photographs, and digitally created collages. The collages incorporate elements from the artist's oil paintings and photography, as well as images created using computer painting and special effects programs. His latest artistic project is live video performances as a VJ. Playing live on a keyboard with special effects capabilities, Carl turns his artwork into fantastic music synchronized videos that are projected unto full-sized movie screens.

An experienced theatrical designer, Carl also has produced many backdrops and scenery for theatre and movie companies. His commissions include a series of murals created for the Universal Pictures movie, *Kindergarten Cop*, starring Arnold Schwartznegger. The murals, created under the artistic direction of Academy Award winning production designer Bruno Rubeo, were used in Universal Picture's worldwide advertising campaign for the movie.

Carl is also an award winning broadcast journalist and news director, and an author of books and essays on a variety of topics. In his multi-faceted life, Carl has worked as a corporate training and development director, as executive director for theater companies and for social service agencies dedicated to helping address the issues of domestic and gang violence.

Visit Carl's website:

www.carllylejenkins.com